Making the Grade

Making the Grade

Reimagining the Graduate Seminar Essay in Literary Studies

Edited by
Kevin A. Morrison

ROWMAN & LITTLEFIELD
Lanham • Boulder • New York • London

Published by Rowman & Littlefield
An imprint of The Rowman & Littlefield Publishing Group, Inc.
4501 Forbes Boulevard, Suite 200, Lanham, Maryland 20706
www.rowman.com

6 Tinworth Street, London SE11 5AL, United Kingdom

Copyright © 2021 by Kevin A. Morrison

All rights reserved. No part of this book may be reproduced in any form or by any electronic or mechanical means, including information storage and retrieval systems, without written permission from the publisher, except by a reviewer who may quote passages in a review.

British Library Cataloguing in Publication Information Available

Library of Congress Cataloging-in-Publication Data

Names: Morrison, Kevin A., 1976- editor.
Title: Making the grade : reimagining the graduate seminar essay / edited by Kevin A. Morrison.
Other titles: Making the grade (Rowman and Littlefield, Inc.)
Description: Lanham, Maryland : Rowman & Littlefield, 2021. | Includes bibliographical references and index. | Summary: "This book is a great resource for new graduate students interested in knowing how to navigate their studies more effectively and creatively"— Provided by publisher.
Identifiers: LCCN 2021009843 (print) | LCCN 2021009844 (ebook) | ISBN 9781475856378 (cloth) | ISBN 9781475856385 (paperback) | ISBN 9781475856392 (epub)
Subjects: LCSH: Universities and colleges—United States—Graduate work—Handbooks, manuals, etc. | Seminars—United States—Handbooks, manuals, etc. | Essay—Authorship—Handbooks, manuals, etc. | Academic writing—Handbooks, manuals, etc.
Classification: LCC LB2371.4 .M35 2021 (print) | LCC LB2371.4 (ebook) | DDC 378.1/55—dc23
LC record available at https://lccn.loc.gov/2021009843
LC ebook record available at https://lccn.loc.gov/2021009844

Contents

Introduction: The Graduate Classroom Staple   1
Kevin A. Morrison

PART I: THE SEMINAR PAPER: HISTORY, CONCEPTION, AND EXPERIENCE   11

1. Essaying Assessment and Assessing the Essay: The Graduate Seminar Paper as Disciplinary Performance   13
Philip Robinson-Self

2. The Cost of Ambiguity: How Students Experience the Graduate Seminar Paper Genre   27
Gabriel Morrison and Thomas Deans

PART II: ARGUMENT, ETHOS, AND INTERVENTION   41

3. The Seminar Essay as Academic Literary Criticism: Strategies for Entering the Scholarly Conversation   43
Almas Khan

4. Writing with Authority: Ethos and the Seminar Essay   57
Elizabeth Vogel

5. A Scaffold for Scholarship: Revising the Seminar Writing Assignment   61
Janet G. Auten

PART III: READING, WRITING, REVISION, AND PRESENTATION — 73

6 Setting Up for Success: Strategies for Managing Research and Writing — 75
   Marilyn Gray

7 Time Management Is Everything: Useful Tips for Graduate Students — 89
   Natalie M. Dorfeld

8 Peer Review, Revisited: Graduate Writing Groups — 99
   Mark Celeste

9 Presenting Research Ideas in a Seminar Setting — 115
   Lucinda Becker

PART IV: NEW DIRECTIONS AND EXPANDING POSSIBILITIES — 131

10 Digital Methods and Visual Essays in the Classroom — 133
   Lisann Anders

11 Structural Shifts and the Graduate Literary Essay: Examples for the Twenty-First-Century Classroom — 149
   Shanthini Pillai

12 Not for Everyone: Experiments in Assessment — 163
   Kevin A. Morrison

Coda: Demystifying the Seminar Paper — 179
Jessie Reeder

References — 185

Index — 195

Contributors — 199

About the Editor — 201

Introduction
The Graduate Classroom Staple
Kevin A. Morrison

This is a book for writers and readers of the graduate-level seminar essay in literary studies. A ubiquitous feature of graduate programs in literature-based disciplines, seminar papers serve as an important first step on a student's path toward undertaking a dissertation and, perhaps, an academic career. Yet it remains a peculiarly understudied genre of professional writing. There has not been, until now, a book devoted solely to its study.

As the first collection to provide sustained attention to the seminar paper as a serious object of study, *Making the Grade: Reimagining the Graduate Seminar Essay in Literary Studies* offers both theoretical reflection and practical advice. In so doing, the essays in this volume explore the following questions:

- What is the history of the seminar paper?
- What purpose(s) does it serve?
- For those who undertake the task of writing a seminar paper, how can they craft arguments on the basis of a single semester's worth of reading?
- How can they speak with confidence and authority?
- For those teachers of graduate seminars, is the article-length paper an appropriate method of assessment for all students who enroll?
- Must the seminar essay assume only one form, or is a variety of formats possible?

AN ESSAY OF "PUBLISHABLE QUALITY"

Graduate-level seminars in literary studies vary widely in form, substance, and terminology. Some are taught on a ten-week quarter system. Others unfold over semesters or terms of thirteen to fifteen weeks. Depending on the national context, those enrolled in a seminar may be called—and call themselves—graduate or postgraduate students. In some countries, where the research-based model dominates, graduate-level seminars are an exception and offered only in a small number of taught MA or PhD programs. In other countries, which follow the taught degree program model, all PhD and MA students will pass through an initial stage of disciplinary seminars.

The demographic makeup of the graduate seminar classroom—from institution to institution and from country to country—has considerable variation as well. Some seminars may include a mix of MA and PhD students, or, depending on the program, maybe solely devoted to the training of either MA or PhD students. At some universities, particularly accomplished or ambitious undergraduates, who are often enrolled in department distinction or university-wide honors programs, may enroll in graduate seminars as well.

Although the term *seminar* may suggest a small cohort of students engaged in rigorous intellectual exchange and lively debate, modes of instruction and class size do, in fact, differ. While discussion is almost always a component of seminars, some professors, believing themselves to be solely responsible for dispensing the course content, will spend the majority of each class session lecturing and responding to students' questions. This may not quite amount to "principling" students—the term John Stuart Mill (after John Locke) uses in his discussion of pedagogues, whose approach emphasizes passive learning—but it does come close.

Other professors will more typically employ one or a combination of formats. Many want students to formulate their independent judgments of the material through discussion with their peers. Professors may, therefore, attempt to frame the discussion by providing opening comments, leading short reading exercises, or facilitating an analysis of visual materials focusing on key themes or concepts. The responsibility of facilitating discussion of the day's readings, however, often falls to students, who work either individually or in pairs (see Steen et al. 1999)

Seminar requirements are equally diverse. Some entail oral presentations and a series of papers designed to introduce students to the shorter professional genres, such as the book review or the conference paper. Professors may expect students to complete one-page summaries and analyses of assigned texts. If the focus of the seminar is organized according to a comprehensively defined field or period, such as Renaissance literature or the Victorian Age, the bulk of the reading list will comprise primary sources from that era. If the seminar is thematic, addressing a topic, movement, critical problem, or genre, the readings will include a great number of secondary sources that hail from different disciplines, such as history, geography, or philosophy.

For all their differences, however, graduate-level seminars in literature—and indeed across the humanities and many social science disciplines—are remarkably similar. Over a defined term, students will read a large number of texts, analyze this material in class, and write a substantial final paper. While professors may take into consideration a student's participation in discussions as well as any other formal and informal assignments, the final paper will, in most cases, constitute the majority of the seminar grade.

Some professors think of the seminar paper as apprentice work. Because it is the one assignment that most closely resembles the forms of professional writing—such as dissertations, scholarly articles, and monographs—where originality of thought and clarity of expression are necessary, these professors see the seminar paper as a task for the student to master. Having to write a number of essays enables one to gain research experience, important conceptual and rhetorical skills, as well as the confidence and authority to speak on a set of issues. While they may be delighted if the essay turns out to be of professional quality, these professors do not expect it.

Most, however, understand that the reality of the job market necessitates that students approach the seminar paper as groundwork for scholarly publishing. In fact, many professors include the specification in their syllabi that the seminar paper be of "publishable quality." This language is no doubt anxiety-inducing. And for good reason: seminar papers written by students with relatively little knowledge about the field or topic, often on a text they have only read once, within an extremely limited timeframe, and routinely under less than ideal conditions—such as having to complete comparable assignments for several different seminars while also, perhaps, teaching—are never publishable.

WHAT PUBLISHABLE QUALITY MEANS

When professors use the phrase *publishable quality*, they do not, in fact, usually mean what they say. Instead, the phrase is intended to signal to students that the final essay should resemble a scholarly article typical of the discipline. At their best, seminar essays, like the published articles on which they are modeled, demonstrate a student's ability to conceptualize a research problem, utilize textual evidence to support a significant thesis, and position oneself intellectually and theoretically by drawing on a variety of secondary sources.

Indeed, in evaluating an essay, professors seek to determine whether the writer possesses the capacity for original research and skillful interpretation. To do so, they will look for at least some of the following qualities in a paper: linkages to an ongoing scholarly discussion or debate (perhaps a provocative attempt to start a conversation or to revive a now dormant one); nimble research skills; logical coherence; clear and effective presentation; and what is sometimes referred to as conceptual self-reflexivity, or the ability to locate oneself intellectually and to define the significant terms and theoretical premises that inform one's work.

The most successful essays may very well have an afterlife as a journal article or a dissertation chapter. They could even serve as the nucleus for a book project down the line. Almost invariably, however, essays are never of publishable quality when they are first submitted to a professor in fulfillment of the requirements of a seminar. To assist students in getting published, most graduate programs now provide at least some level of training in writing and revising practice.

These efforts range on a spectrum from formal to informal. On the one hand, some institutions have established Graduate Writing Centers or incorporated tutorial support for graduate students within centers that largely cater to the undergraduate population (Lawrence and Zawacki 2019). Universities and specific graduate programs now offer workshops and seminars that are specifically designed to help students revise an essay to make it suitable for publication. These occasional events on scholarly writing may be included in a series that focuses on different aspects of a student's professional development or on the fundamentals of an academic career covering such topics as archival research, effective time management, and conference applications and presentations.

On the other hand, an increasing number of graduate programs in literature has devoted formal curricular space to professional writing.[1] These stand-alone optional or required courses appear under an assortment of names that range from the descriptive ("Academic Writing Workshop") to the indicative ("Writing for Publication") to the pithy ("Project Publish"). Depending on a given program's requirements—which can include one to three years of coursework, comprehensive and field-specific examinations, and the writing of a prospectus and, ultimately, a dissertation—the writing seminar may be taken in a student's third, fourth, or even fifth year.

Writing seminars are usually led by a single faculty member who oversees students' revisions and provides advice on selecting appropriate journals. Although it is common for these seminars to follow a workshop format in which fellow graduate students and the instructor read and evaluate essays collectively, other models exist. In addition to workshopping papers, for example, some professors ask their colleagues to read them under double-anonymous conditions in which the names of the faculty readers and the students are withheld from one another. This provides students with an opportunity to experience their first set of readers' reports, if they have not already submitted an article for publication on their own, and to discuss the best ways forward.

Although ad hoc and informal graduate writing workshops in which peers read and critique each other's work have existed for decades, devoting official curricular space to the development of students' critical writing projects is relatively new. Many departments now recognize that graduate students are unprepared to enter the profession and to face the challenges of an ever-contracting academic job market.

There are a number of valid intellectual reasons for opposing the increasing professionalization of graduate students. In 1994, the then-president of the Modern Language Association (MLA), Patricia Meyer Spacks, caused something of a firestorm when she lamented that students "who concentrate on turning out publishable papers can hardly center their attention on broadening and deepening their knowledge" (Spacks 1994). If students define their specialties and subspecialties too early, so this line of thinking goes, they will miss valuable opportunities for intellectual exploration and to experiment with different methodological approaches.

Such concerns are perfectly reasonable. However, there are numerous other reasons for thinking that the formalization of professional development is warranted. One of the most salutary effects of providing professional training to graduate students has been, for example, to demystify aspects of the academy that are otherwise quite opaque.

THE ESSAY: FOUNDATIONAL BUILDING BLOCK OF AN ACADEMIC CAREER

Before writing an article or a dissertation, the graduate student must first complete several end-of-term essays. This assignment is the fundamental building block of an academic career. As Eric Hayot argues, "one of the most important things you should know how to do, and how to do well, as an academic" is to write an essay (Hayot 2014, 8). And the first move toward mastering the craft is writing essays for graduate seminars.

Yet, there are surprisingly few resources available to students at this stage. Undergraduates in search of advice on planning, writing, and presenting their research can consult any number of handbooks. Graduate students who need guidance on conceptualizing a dissertation or thesis have recourse to dozens of helpful books, including many that feature step-by-step instructions and day-to-day tasks. Newly minted PhDs who aspire to turn their dissertations into books or to publish chapters as articles can consult a plethora of guides to revision and publication.

While the seminar paper is occasionally discussed in works that examine broader issues in the academy, there are remarkably few other resources available.[2] The graduate student looking for advice on how to complete the assignment can glean much helpful information from Alan Durant and Nigel Fabb's *How to Write Essays and Dissertations: A Guide for English Literature Students* (2016). Yet *Making the Grade* is distinct insofar as it addresses itself to both writers and—as the following section of this introduction will discuss—readers of the seminar paper, whereas Durant and Fabb focus solely on writers. Moreover, it focuses solely on the seminar paper, which has a distinct disciplinary history and set of aims from the dissertation.

Introduction 7

In his widely read guide to building an academic career, Gregory Colón Semenza (2010) devotes a chapter to the seminar paper. He takes the reader through each stage of conceiving, researching, writing, and revising it (2010, 90–115). While indebted to Semenza's efforts, this book explores why the seminar paper has become a ubiquitous feature of the graduate classroom, how it is experienced by students who undertake it, and the utility of—and possible adaptations to—the assignment for those who will work outside the academy as well as those who will take up positions in predominantly teaching-focused institutions. Additionally, this volume addresses many new developments in digital media.

Of course, one can also gain important advice from any number of other books devoted to writing for publication. Although these guides are not focused on the seminar paper, they also offer helpful tips on argument, structure, style, time management, note-taking, and organizing research files. However, the demands of a seminar essay are different from those of writing for publication. Students do not have the freedom to identify a topic of interest but must do so within the given parameters of a course. They usually conceive the topic and write these essays in the final weeks of term. They are not likely to have access to archives or specialist libraries and must make do with the institutional resources available to them.

A BOOK FOR READERS OF SEMINAR ESSAYS TOO

Thus far, the focus in this introduction has been on writers of seminar papers. But the essays in this collection are also concerned with readers—that is, with professors who utilize the graduate essay assignment in their classrooms. Professors are, with very few exceptions, not trained to teach graduate students and simply replicate the experiences they had as graduate students.

They may not stop to ask, therefore, whether the seminar essay is always the most effective assignment. Indeed, to the extent that seminar essays are only assumed to offer training for the writing of dissertation chapters and critical articles, other considerations are often occluded. Many graduate students will move into teaching positions on the so-called educator track or in teaching streams in which research may be of secondary importance. Does the emphasis on the essay in graduate seminars help to prepare those individuals for their careers?

In fact, the graduate classroom includes a greater mix of students than the assignment might imply. Aspiring literary scholars and cultural historians sit alongside future policy analysts, lawyers, deans of students, acquisitions editors, and secondary school teachers. How might seminar papers prepare graduate students for careers in non-university settings? Because many professors in MA- or PhD-granting institutions expect their students to follow their lead and pursue a similar path, the utility of the seminar essay is rarely conceived or discussed in terms of those who, by choice or circumstance, move outside the academy.

Certainly, as some of the contributors to this volume argue, thinking of the seminar essay as a skills-based assignment can be beneficial. After all, in order to write an effective seminar essay, a student must define a complex project and seek to execute it within a limited timeframe; organize and carry out research; work independently while heeding a supervisor's advice; and, ideally, undertake substantial revision. The PhD or MA in literary studies may not be a transferable academic credential—insofar as it does not certify one for a career outside of the discipline—but the skills gained along the way can be beneficial in a number of different contexts.

Making the Grade takes up questions about the utility of the graduate essay from diverse vantage points. From clarifying the purpose of the essay and its stakes to incorporating visual elements to offering the assignment as one option among several, contributors to this volume seek to imagine this longstanding staple of the graduate classroom anew.

OVERVIEW

In short, this book is for anyone who wonders how this assignment has gained such prominence in graduate-level instruction and how it might be utilized in rapidly changing literature-based disciplines. It is for professors of literature who teach graduate students, as well as graduate students in MA and PhD programs requiring coursework, throughout the English-speaking world. It is also for graduate students and professors in writing and rhetoric departments and those whose teaching and research interests include writing and pedagogy.

Contributing broadly to the scholarship of teaching and learning while focusing narrowly on the genre of the seminar paper, the book is divided into four parts:

- Part I, "The Seminar Paper: History, Conception, and Experiences," examines the emergence and protocols of the genre and surveys some of the ways students understand (or are confused about) the assignment today.
- Part II, "Argument, Ethos, and Intervention," provides practical advice on how to frame and deliver an argument while entering into a critical conversation.
- Part III, "Reading, Writing, Revision, and Presentation," focuses on effective research strategies, time management, and utilizing the feedback of one's peers.
- Part IV, "New Directions, and Expanding Possibilities," considers ways that the assignment, although still a staple of the graduate classroom, is changing.

A coda offers personal reflections by one professor of how she experienced the essay assignment as a graduate student and how she teaches it today.

In addition to the book you hold in your hands, you will find additional resources, discussion, and insight at gradseminar.com.

NOTES

1. On the need for such formalized efforts, see Micciche and Carr 2011.
2. Pugh and Johnson (2014) make the case for writing as one of the many critical skills that graduate programs should cultivate. Wallack (2017) insists on the centrality of essays in the intellectual development of students and teachers. Cassuto (2015) reflects on the efficacy of writing seminar papers as part of a larger analysis of graduate student training.

Part I

THE SEMINAR PAPER

HISTORY, CONCEPTION, AND EXPERIENCE

Chapter 1

Essaying Assessment and Assessing the Essay

The Graduate Seminar Paper as Disciplinary Performance

Philip Robinson-Self

Confusing, daunting, exhilarating, mysterious, masterful: the range of adjectives one can throw at the seminar essay as a piece of assessment is as varied as the range of responses one feels as a student or academic in attempting to write or to grade them. With these responses as background, this chapter begins by providing a brief overview of the development of the essay. It then charts some of the challenges to the essay's use as a form of assessment and the difficulties students face in achieving its objectives, arguing for ways in which these obstacles may be overcome.

It is important, however, to begin with something of a reminder: essays are not simply formal or mechanical compositions but rather complex interactions among author, readers, and contexts, in their own way as important and dynamic as the subjects they analyze. While this account and this way of seeing the essay stem from my own discipline of literary studies, it is nonetheless applicable across the arts and humanities and may well resonate beyond; such an account, one might argue, is bound up in the history of the essay as an intellectual construct.

(PRE)HISTORIES OF THE ESSAY

As a piece of assessment, the graduate seminar essay remains ubiquitous across arts and humanities, with a seminar paper of one form or another as the culminating point for the vast majority of graduate courses (Semenza 2010, 90). Indeed, the seminar and its product have been seen as "the two dominant signature pedagogies at the heart of English doctoral study" (Khost et al. 2015, 20). Simultaneously, the idea of the essay as a form of assessment, its legitimacy, is increasingly under threat; in some respects, perhaps rightly so.

For many years, educational innovation from various ends of the sector and beyond has striven to convince us that new modes of assessment can more effectively drive, and more accurately measure, student learning. The sort of learning that takes place in the seminar could, we are told, be more accurately, more meaningfully, and more usefully assessed by multimedia presentation, group work, online portfolio, book review, creative report, reflective memoir, news article, and so on.

By comparison, the traditional essay, like the traditional lecture, is often viewed as an antiquated model in need of resuscitation or replacement as a mode of assessment. And certainly, the essay has a long enough pedigree within and without the walls of universities; importantly, the impacts of both strands of its historical practice have a continued bearing on its present use. Before turning in more detail to the arguments one can make against and for the essay form, then, it is worth remembering where it has come from and how this history is still enshrined in the expectations of the form today.

The usual point of departure for histories of the essay is to reference late sixteenth-century (Western) Europe. Perhaps unsurprisingly, Michel de Montaigne and Francis Bacon tend to loom large in such discussions, where they are often linked with ideas of the essay as being originally a kind of loose, draft work (Andrews 2003, Badley 2010, Gigante 2014). Arguments for the status of the essay as originally an informal gesture are regularly rooted in discussions of these two foundational figures, legitimizing an impression of "the provisional, speculative nature of the genre, the suggestion of a test, a tryout" (Wood 2014, 1).

Similarly the *Oxford English Dictionary* (*OED*), which in providing its definition of "essay" as an "action or process of trying or testing" touches on the (more or less obsolete) sense of "trial, testing, proof, experiment" comparable with the French *essai*. The *OED* quotes from Bacon's *Advancement of Learning* (1605) as the primary example, in a discussion in which the physical universe is regarded as "able to maintain itself to infinite essaies or proofes of Nature."

Though the *OED* has no space to dwell on such things, we might note that essays or proofs seem here to be offered not quite as alternatives but perhaps as something approaching synonyms; this is worth bearing in mind because it resists the determination that the (Baconian, at least) essay is strictly provisional, unscientific, or otherwise methodologically loose. The *OED* writes off the essay form itself as "a composition of moderate length . . . originally implying want of finish." Both Montaigne and Bacon are relied on as origin points for this meaning, in a tradition which feels oddly dismissive of the essay form.

Admittedly, both Montaigne's *Essais* (1580) and Bacon's *Essayes* (1597) initially look loose in design and execution: Womack voices tradition in arguing that for both authors the essay "was a deliberate suspension of rhetorical formality," a sketch, draft, or personal monologue "enjoying the freedom of a bracketed and unofficial discourse" (Womack 1993, 43). But it might also be said, probably for Montaigne and almost certainly for Bacon, that appearances can be deceiving.

Montaigne's short prefacing argument to the reader that he would in his work write "sans estude et artifice" (without study or artifice) belies the rhetorical work of his three volumes, and his own conception of the subject as "si frivole et si vain" (so frivolous and vain) equally belies the remarkable intellectual drive and curiosity which fuels the work (Montaigne 2007, 27). Meanwhile, Bacon's essays, whether in the 1597 version (ten essays), the enlarged 1612 edition (thirty-eight essays), or the again enlarged 1625 edition (fifty-eight essays), are scrupulously considered.

While many of these essays were altered or expanded in the later editions, this does not quite imply the status of drafting so much as Bacon's careful and decidedly politic response to a very quickly changing world. Some of the essays are short, some longer, some argumentative, some deliberative, some epigrammatic, from deeply metaphorical to glaringly literal, "curiosity cabinets of finely polished gems in pointed rhetorical style" (Gigante 2010, 554).

Bacon's essays, then, are sallies, something to excite readers and draw them into a particular subject. If they imply a want of finish, then it is by design. What makes the essay an essay for Bacon is not in and of itself a matter of style but of purpose, the staking out of a (considered, systematic, philosophical) intellectual position in relation to a miscellany of subject matters. The sense of overall purpose in the collection evolved over time. All the same, Bacon's *Essayes* might be said to remain Bacon's *Essayes*, whether the printing contains ten or fifty-eight of them.

Indeed, seminal work by Ronald Crane (1968) long ago pointed out that the miscellany of Bacon's work may not be miscellaneous in design, that the subjects of many of the essays in both the 1612 and 1625 editions are not randomly chosen but actively work to fill in gaps in knowledge asserted by the scientific program set out in *The Advancement of Learning*. Whether the essays quite succeed in this goal, or indeed if their goal is even to succeed per se, remains a subject for debate.

Still, what is certain is that, like many a good student, Bacon's ambition evolved along with his confidence in the utility of the form; by 1625 he could write of his work, with typical assurance, that "I doe conceive, that the Latine Volume of them (being in the Universall Language) may last, as long as Bookes last" (Bacon 1625, A3v-A4r). Whatever one makes of Bacon's decided sense of self-worth, it is clear that this is neither draft work nor precisely a trial of anything (except, perhaps, of the reader's capacity to put up with him).

An appreciation of Bacon's and Montaigne's place in the history of the essay is important not because they represent an origin point but rather because they do not, or at least not quite. There have occasionally been debates about exactly how much of an influence Montaigne's work was on Bacon's design, but it seems clear that Bacon rested on Montaigne, and both rested heavily on the classics: Aristotle, Plutarch, Lucretius, and Seneca (and both, too, were in debt to Erasmus).

Both, equally, had somewhat mixed feelings about this heritage. Montaigne, for example, "often expressed his hostility to classical rhetoric ... but the way in which he used his reading and developed his arguments owes everything to his grammar-school training" (Mack 2010, 1). There are differences in approach despite shared learning: Montaigne is conversational in tone, even humorous; Bacon is more insistent, more serious, and less personal. Still, despite differences in style, both are working within a recognizable, evolving genre of activity.

Though Bacon stands out to us in his particular molding of the form, expository prose was nonetheless a common enough feature of the period. Even then, compositions were bewilderingly varied in subject scope (Black 2006, 1). Very soon after Montaigne and Bacon, we can list the essays of

William Cornwallis (meditative), John Stephens (ironical and instructive), Alexander Craig (poetic), George Wither (satirical), and Daniel Turill (politic and moral).

These writers all borrowed the word for their titles but can hardly be said to have learned how to write essays overnight; they were already thinking, reading, and writing in a tradition. In the centuries following, a canonical continuum of the essay would list luminaries such as Addison, Steele, or Johnson, for whom the essay was famously "an irregular undigested piece" and "a loose sally of the mind," definitions which, as with the titling of Johnson's *Rambler* or *Idler* periodicals, again belie the level of intellectual investment in the project.

And while it has become commonplace to chart the journey of the essay with high points (eighteenth-century treatise) and low points (nineteenth-century belletrist), such sweeping histories obscure both important commonalities and important differences in approach and which are the highs and which the lows rather depends on who, or what academic discipline, one asks. We might better understand the essay as an assessment by thinking about its cultural development and its attachment to particular modes of thought.

Just so for the emergence of the essay in education. In grammar schools, practice in rhetorical exercises (*progymnasmata* in ancient Greek) taught and assessed the skills of composition and argumentation early on (Clark 2006). Universities took a bit longer to fully embrace written work. Traditionally oral and disputational in nature, the examinations of the universities had from the medieval period included written elements (the scriptum), but it was not until the eighteenth and nineteenth centuries that the weighting of examination switched heavily toward written assessment (Clark 2006, 139).

There were a number of reasons for this evolution, from the bureaucratic to the more pedagogic, but one important element that stands out and which seriously impacts the use of the essay as assessment today is the connection with the rise of empire and colonialism. After all, the emergence of the English civics, institutions that came to be known as redbrick universities, took place at the height of the British Empire and was explicitly aimed at serving a rapidly industrializing, globalizing society.

As with the growth of Oxford and Cambridge in the Tudor period, an expanding state was in need of educated workers, officials, and bureaucrats. For that matter, in terms of Britain's global interests, it was also in need of examinations which could be implemented at a distance and in large numbers. The examined essay increasingly became used as not simply an assessment of knowledge but of character (Clark 2006).

This was thought to be important for those in dependent territories, fulfilling much the same function, and with much the same glaring moral and practical problems, as a citizenship test attempts today. This preoccupation with character lasted "across more than a century," and one can argue that essays have remained fundamentally moralistic as an assessment (Womack 1993, 45).

At the same time, the development of the essay as an expected product of those in higher education also evolved hand in hand with the development of the seminar as a formal structure of higher education. Travelling from the Humboldtian, Prussian concept of university education to the United States, the seminar quickly became the organizational principle of institutional life. By the end of the nineteenth century, the seminar was perceived at Columbia University as "the wheel within the wheel, the real center of the life-giving, the stimulating, the creative forces of the modern university" (Clark 2006, 141).

The seminar has gone from strength to strength, becoming "the mainstay of graduate education" and the essay its dominant product (Khost et al. 2015, 20). Hence the essay as an assessment rests on a dual, linked history: the global spread of research-oriented liberal education and the lasting effects of cultural imperialism. The essay is, then, not a morbid relic of the university's past but part and parcel of its rise to global prominence.

After all, when Bacon wrote that the "Latine Volume" of his *Essayes* would last "as long as Bookes last," he was right about the longevity of the essays but wrong about the longevity of Latin as the language of transmission. The logical manner of an essay's argument is not simply natural, it is a logic specific to Western philosophy and particularly to Anglophone cultural history; its structures of progression, persuasion, defense, and evidence, or of thesis, antithesis, and synthesis are particular to developments in Western intellectual thought.

The voice of the essay, distant, rational, and experienced, is that of a humanist tradition: "it is supported by a belief that discourse in words is important, and that the presentation and exchange of ideas is fundamental to human civilised discourse" (Andrews 2003, 119). This particularity, this history remains bound up in the expectations of the essay today. It is no exaggeration to say that every time we read, write, or grade an essay, we take part in the reproduction and performance of these histories; if we are only dimly aware of that past, what impact might this have on the quality or meaningfulness of our performance?

ESSAYING ASSESSMENT

Essays, therefore, have a complex history. They are in themselves a perplexing mix of practice and product. That is not, of course, a new observation. Dealing with the contradictory, the puzzling, they have long frustrated scholarly enquiry; John McCarthy described the essay as "that enigmatic and elusive genre which seems to defy definition," while Claire de Obaldia's landmark work found the nature of the essay to be "the most reflexive and critical in that it constantly questions its own form" (McCarthy 1989, ix; Obaldia 1995, 23).

Calling on the formidable intellectual energies of theorists from Georg Lukács to Theodor Adorno to Max Bense, the question of the essay has become something of a long-standing crux. In a similar vein, essayists themselves from William Cornwallis through Ralph Waldo Emerson through Aldous Huxley have regularly stopped to pause over exactly what their writing might be.

It puzzled Virginia Woolf, for whom the essay's glittering variety could be "about God and Spinoza, or about turtles and Cheapside," just as much as it did G. K. Chesterton, whose sense of the "elusive nature" of the essay as a "leap in the dark" led him to conclude, with some justification alongside the hyperbole, that the "perfect essay has never been written" (Woolf 1994, 216; Chesterton 2000, 17).

As a form "more concerned with becoming than being" (Gigante 2010, 564n), the essay in English is both a frustrated search for meaningful truth and a highly creative work; it is therefore balanced between the intellectual structures and aesthetic norms of fact and fiction. This balancing act, the essay's vibrant, elusive nature, is one of the real joys of working in the form. But if such a careful, indeed problematic balance can try the imagination of its most brilliant practitioners, it is hardly a surprise that it necessarily leads to a number of problems when the essay is assessed.

Some of the questions asked of the essay as university assessment are fairer than others. On a practical level, how well does the essay prepare students for life beyond higher education? After all, the essay as a format of assessment reproduces a poetics which can also be read as neither one thing nor the other: "it has neither a clear practical function . . . nor, on the other hand, the conventions of literature (like a poem or a novel)" (Womack 1993, 44). For those increasing numbers of students who do not remain in academia, we might make clearer the use-value of twenty-page seminar papers on relatively esoteric subjects.

In written assessment, book reviews, archival projects, critical editions, conference papers, and the like, all look more immediately useful and more immediately authentic than the essay. For that matter, such assessments can also incorporate technology or multimedia learning in a way the traditional essay cannot. This all assumes, of course, that we accept the (not unproblematic) idea that higher education is about preparing students for working life after graduation, rather than a liberal end in and of itself.

The graduate seminar essay, at least, can make some claim to fulfilling both ambitions, preparing students for life as a researcher and (to a lesser extent) teacher, but even here it can fall short. Seminar essays do not by and large purport to be pieces of original research and tend to stress overall knowledge of a given area rather than degrees of specialism or push toward subject (re)definition.

It is also the case that, as many have pointed out, preparing students primarily for entry into work in higher education when there are not enough jobs available to fulfill that goal is both illogical and fairly pernicious (Cassuto 2015). But for those remaining in academia, too, the excesses of the graduate essay can sometimes raise problems. The drive for publishable quality as the goal of good writing "compels junior scholars to try to publish too early, too often, and too theoretically for anyone to keep up, or even want to keep up, with what is produced" (Khost et al. 2015, 21).

A publishable piece is not something that is put together overnight, nor ideally in the short space of a busy semester. Little wonder that it should challenge students. That challenge carries real weight: the essay, like any assessment on which a good part of a student's grade depends, is high stakes. It is high stakes in practical terms but also intellectually and emotionally in exposing a detailed view of a subject to someone who is in all likelihood more knowledgeable in that view.

On both sides of the Atlantic, graduate courses are short compared to the years spent as an undergraduate or writing a thesis. They are also intense. Students are expected to grapple with multiple new ways of thinking in a compressed space of time. Alongside the increased difficulty is sometimes a dangerous sense that graduate students possess an innate improved ability over undergraduates (Khost et al. 2015, 19). These assumptions are damaging, even for those students who are more adept in the subject.

There are questions to be asked at a deeper level. How well does the essay, a form for many centuries the more or less exclusive province of white and relatively wealthy European men, cope with intersectionality, queer discourse, race, disability, or cultural difference? As university cohorts increasingly expand and diversify, there is a concomitant push to reflect broader participation within curricula.

It is clear that universities are under increased calls to recognize and make amends for their masculine, imperialist origins, whether this is expressed by the University of Manchester's replacement of Kipling with Maya Angelou, the Rhodes Must Fall movement, or a call for the inclusion of female scholars among the marble sculptures of men that line the Long Room library at Trinity College Dublin.

The essay cannot easily put aside its history as an assessment predicated on the expansion of English and of English definitions of good writing. In theory, the versatility of the essay would allow diversity of voice; in practice, the voice required, the voice built into the idea of the essay, can remain suspiciously akin to the rarefied, rational, and artificially detached air of the Edwardian period (Sambell et al. 2013, 17).

Essay writing hence might be said to replicate structures of power to which its range of authors has at best unequal access. Whether they are written within the context of an assessment or not, essays "are credentialing displays of erudition," and erudition is more or less in the eye and ear of the beholder (Jones 2018, 222). This makes the essay inherently inequitable; even for those of us who might have some claim to cultural access to essay writing as a form (university educated, Anglophone, and middle class), it remains a difficult enterprise.

Faced with the difficulty involved in making use of this form to express complex arguments, students may instead fall back on imitation and regurgitation of information (Sambell et al. 2013, 17). Indeed, as the culminating act of a seminar, the seminar paper implicitly (and sometimes explicitly) asks students to demonstrate learning by imitation of the sort of scholarship they have read, rather than by synthesis or origination.

The complexities of academic writing and rhetoric are to a certain extent reflected in the broad scope of composition classes in the United States and the increasing scope of academic literacies in the UK. However, despite the clamor from writing centers that for such support to be meaningful, it ought to be embedded in, or otherwise offered in concert with, academic disciplines; it has become all too easy to view writing support in terms of a deficit model, a place to send students when their writing is not up to scratch.

Taking this approach rarely solves the problem, or even properly recognizes the issues involved; it reduces writing to the status of a generalizable skill that can be divorced from disciplinary context and risks rendering the intellectual work involved in writing invisible (Mitchell 2010, 135). Certainly, students might be better prepared for and supported in approaching the essay. Most students, even at the graduate level, will struggle with fully independent work as an alternative to the passive, accumulative, and dependent experiences of learning with which they may be most familiar (Jones 2018, 229).

This is, perhaps, particularly the case with the seminar paper, where the independence is extended and the expectations are notoriously diverse:

> For most graduate students, confronting the seminar paper each semester is akin to launching an arctic expedition without a compass or a map; you may have some sense of where you want to go but painfully little guidance about how to get there. (Semenza 2010, 90)

There is no one conception of what the seminar essay should look like, either across disciplines or within them.

This leaves students to the difficult and somewhat thankless task of managing the particularity of subject epistemologies and a variety of tutorial expectations (Hodgson and Harris 2013, 7). An essay simply does not mean the same thing in aims, construction, or tone in English Literature as it does in History; both will be different from an essay in Philosophy. This creates serious problems for students travelling from one discipline to another, but it also raises issues within those disciplines themselves; we might be more active in terms of rendering visible the particular character of writing in our respective fields.

All this begins to look like the essay is not merely unserviceable but actively sinister. "If you take a conspiracy view of affairs," Richard Andrews writes, "you might say that the centrality of the essay in the academy is a subtly insidious form of gatekeeping" (Andrews 2003, 119). Our standards are not always clearly apparent, nor are the histories that underwrite those standards always as legible as they might be.

For all these reasons, essays, in addition to their other problems, have become particularly sensitive to questions of attribution. The activities of essay mills, though inflated by areas of government and media increasingly eager to find fault with higher education, are nonetheless worrying. The answer, and it may be a somewhat knee-jerk answer, has been in some cases not to use the essay at all; some universities will not allow courses to be assessed by essays alone, precisely because of perceived difficulties in definitively attributing the work to its stated author.

However, academic studies of plagiarism tend to show the concept as complex and contested. While plagiarism may come about as a result of unfamiliarity with relatively banal issues such as citation style, it may also be a result of more significant difficulties with the nature of academic discourse. Avoiding the very assessment which exposes and surfaces such difficulties denies opportunities for valuable learning on all sides and risks sidestepping important issues.

If there are problems in the utilization of the essay, then, these are not necessarily problems with the essay itself so much as one visible encounter with underlying concerns in graduate education: with discourse, disciplinarity, the character of knowledge, and the nature of universities. In that case, conceptual and practical difficulties may point to a real continuing value in the essay. As both assessment and cultural product, the essay binds up a number of issues inherent in the current life of universities and offers a tool with which to confront and explore these areas; this angle is pursued in concluding this chapter.

ESSAYS AS DISCIPLINARY PERFORMANCE

As an assessment, the essay as currently performed may have serious shortcomings in terms of validity, reliability, authenticity, equity, transparency, and attribution (though it is not alone in that). And yet it is, this chapter contends, the single most important intellectual tool that can be given to students. Crafting such essays initiates students into the language games of our chosen disciplines (Badley 2010), and the more essays written, the deeper that engagement becomes.

When students write essays, they are not merely attempting pieces of assessment but are learning to speak, to think in, the language of the discipline. In other words, they are learning what Bourdieu (1977) influentially termed the habitus of the particular field. But in taking an active approach to essaying, they also have the opportunity to impact that field, to assume a position of real agency in relation to their subject.

When instructors ask students to write essays, they are inviting them with various degrees of specificity to take an active role within the history sketched out in the first section of this chapter and to take an active stake in relation to the issues set out in the second section. That is not always a terribly clear or easy task: the essay asks for its student writers to adopt the inherently problematic position of authorship, of an authoritative voice, concerning a subject on which they are not (or at least not initially) authoritative.

As has been pointed out, that is something of a double bind peculiar to the essay, combining the drive and thirst for knowledge, the not-knowing that is characteristic of the form, with the assumed pretense, also characteristic of the form, of adopting a persona that does know (Womack 1993, 47; Robertson 2014, 263). The voice of the essay is authoritative, deliberative; that authority is also always to some extent an act, a role play. But when we are honest about the challenges in assuming that conflicted authorial position, challenge can also more obviously become opportunity.

Firstly, the opportunity to intervene in and to shape academic discourse: academic writing is always an active process, "a problematical and tentative exercise in critical reflective thinking" (Badley 2009, 219). Secondly, the essay offers the opportunity to shape the wider intellectual, disciplinary spaces in which such discourse takes place. Not only a great essay but every essay is involved in researching, representing, and reshaping the subjects it writes; essays are not simply a form or mode for the reiteration of knowledge but are "engines for *shaping* knowledge" (Jones 2018, 230).

Thirdly, working through our relationship to subjects in extended essays offers the opportunity to shape ourselves and to hone our own critical voice;

more broadly, it offers a means through which to think through our sense of self. In a way, that gets us back to a key character-forming purpose in universities, if in a more individualistic and representative fashion, where the university offers "critical spaces where we might shape and re-shape ourselves" (Badley 2009, 215).

All those opportunities speak to the lasting values acquired from study in the humanities: criticality, self-authorship, meta-learning, and the ability "to discern ways . . . to learn anew and to reflect" (Jones 2018, 230). Revealing those opportunities while teaching students through the attendant challenges necessarily requires something of a change in perspective. Students struggle to achieve an authoritative voice partly because they are shown a great deal of finished work and tend not to be walked through the processes, visions, and revisions that produced such work.

Teaching the essay as process, taking students through the steps performed in constructing them, would offer a better grasp of those opportunities and joys to be found in writing. This is all particularly true of the graduate seminar essay, where the risks might be said to be higher but the possible rewards higher too. Those twenty-page papers are lengthy for a reason: they offer scope for real freedom.

Giving students the choice, the freedom to approach topics and areas that interest them and to explore them in ways which make sense, to give them the opportunity to present those interests to another (even the assumed other of the essay form), clearly deepens their engagement not merely with the particular assignment, and not merely with university study, but with the fundamental building blocks of the subject.

Being able to play with those blocks offers students the opportunity for agency; here, the essential versatility and flexibility of the essay ensures its longevity, its continued relevance, offering students the space "to inject personal perspectives, to alter the sequence and play with the tone of the genre" (Andrews 2003, 126). Approaching the seminar essay only as a summative assessment performed at the conclusion of a seminar (and criticizing it on this basis) is unhelpfully reductive; instead, the essay should be seen as something which travels with us in our learning.

For students and for academics, the work of the essay is our signature pedagogy and an intimate relation of disciplinary form to disciplinary content: after all, "the 'weighing' of the essay is the activity of criticism itself"

(Gray 1999, 277). Across the arts and humanities we work to understand and express the experience of humanity, we tend to value intellectual complexity, multiplicity, ambiguity, and uncertainty. Those things can be conveyed, captured, and explored in the essay in ways in which they cannot in other forms, precisely because essays have been trying to grasp at complexity for hundreds of years.

A really good seminar paper will (implicitly) understand the histories and complexities of the essay, and in its form, content, and intellectual drive will work to (explicitly) answer them. If the answer surprises us, or is different from an equally good answer we have seen before, then the essay has done its work, as it has been doing for centuries.

Chapter 2

The Cost of Ambiguity
How Students Experience the Graduate Seminar Paper Genre

Gabriel Morrison and Thomas Deans

Graduate students are positioned as apprentices to disciplines, as emerging but not-yet-expert researchers. They are more expert than their professors in at least one area, though: They know their own experience. Gaining access to that experience can be vexing for scholars in literary studies, whose habit is to fix on textual artifacts rather than on thinking processes; however, colleagues in composition studies have long employed empirical methods to capture how writers, especially student writers, perceive contexts and negotiate tasks. Using such methods, in tandem with rhetorical genre studies and a small but growing body of existing research on graduate writers, this chapter documents how one cohort of doctoral students perceives the seminar paper as a genre and as a practice.

As one might expect, we found that graduate writers are anxious, but we also discovered some less expected patterns. Their understandings of *purpose* vary widely; their interactions with *people* significantly shape their understandings of the seminar paper genre; and in the typical seminar, they encounter little explicit guidance in the drafting and revising *process*. Our method here is primarily phenomenological, letting the students speak for themselves as much as possible. In our analysis, we organize participant responses into themes and reflect on our findings. At the end of the chapter, we offer some summary advice as to how graduate programs can use findings from this study to strengthen graduate pedagogy.

To access student perceptions of the seminar paper, we conducted interviews with seven doctoral students in English at a large public research university. We also asked participants to write out a brief, impromptu definition of the seminar paper genre and to share with us one of their recent papers. The cohort was relatively diverse, but all saw themselves on trajectories toward faculty careers. We asked about their lived experiences with the seminar paper genre and used thematic analysis to discern the most salient points of consensus and confusion.

Graduate education has long been of interest to writing researchers as a kind of crucible where people develop advanced and highly specific literate expertise (Berkenkotter et al. 1988; Sullivan 1991; Prior 1998; Ivanič 1998; Lundell and Beach 2003). The expansion of graduate education in recent years (Okahana and Zhou 2018) has led to a wave of new research on graduate writing (Caplan and Cox 2016; Lawrence and Zawacki 2019) as well as the founding of the Consortium on Graduate Communication in 2014. Nearly all of the research in this area affirms that writing in graduate school is a thoroughly social phenomenon that is fraught with complex negotiations of identity and ideology, conflicting understandings of purpose and process, and incremental, nonlinear growth. The liminal nature of graduate writing also creates a paradox:

> On the one hand, the discursive knowledge-making practices that research cultures develop over generations to accomplish their knowledge work become normalized, transparent, invisible, and indeed appear universal to long-term members of research cultures, rendering writing a non-question. On the other hand, for newcomers, these very practices constitute new territory and a vital site of inquiry into how knowledge and researcher identities are produced and negotiated in these research cultures. (Starke-Meyerring 2011, 92)

Our study makes visible how graduate students in English, as newcomers to a research community, negotiate a signature genre.

PURPOSE: "I'M CONFUSED BY THAT CONSTANTLY"

Our interviewees rehearsed the expected features of the seminar paper genre—that it should engage with the "critical conversation" in a given field, that it should make a "critical intervention" and "sustained argument," that it should embrace complexity, that it should run fifteen to twenty-five pages. They often arrived at elegant distillations:

> I know that a seminar paper involves what's going on in the class; what's going on in my head, in terms of, like, where I want to go with my own research; and what the field has to say about the intersection thereof.

But doctoral students said that *purpose* was rarely discussed in their seminars. It was left ambiguous.

When asked directly about the purpose of seminar papers, participants in our study reflexively juxtaposed priorities, often equivocating from one sentence to the next. When asked to write out a definition of the seminar paper, one participant succinctly named the three purposes that compete for primacy:

> A graduate school seminar paper is an impetus to read actively, dive deeply into specific scholarship and lines of inquiry, and to test out synthesizing ideas by putting them on paper. Most basically, a seminar paper satisfies the requirements of any given course. However, the seminar paper is ultimately an opportunity to draft potential articles and/or dissertation chapters.

Learning. Grades. Professionalization. These three motives emerged in various permutations throughout our interviews. The oscillating rankings, often expressed tentatively or nervously, suggest that the governing motive of the seminar essay is anything but settled in the minds of students—or faculty.

Some professors explicitly foregrounded one purpose. Several participants favorably recalled one faculty member who prioritized professionalization and insisted that students see their seminar papers as future conference papers and journal articles. This professor guided students through a progressive, multistage research and writing process, starting early in the semester and always angling toward publication. Even years later, many students remember that process as an exemplar—and as an exception.

Participants more frequently mentioned faculty who instead explicitly prioritized experimentation and learning, giving students license to "practice," to "try things out," to "take a first run at something," to engage in "a learning exercise" without worrying about publishing. Students internalized that priority: "A seminar paper should be the opportunity to try out new ideas/methods/writing about new texts. . . . It should be a space where risk-taking is encouraged." This exploratory, student-centered approach resonates with what writing across the curriculum scholars have long called "writing to learn." It positions the student more as a learner than as a professional, and it is evident in reflections like this one:

> A seminar paper need not be a publishable piece of writing; rather, the goal is to practice developing, sustaining, and defending a critical intervention in an ongoing conversation about relevant questions in the field. Ideally, a seminar paper will also provide students with an opportunity to pursue their own specific interests that they have developed over the course of the semester. A seminar paper will also give students the chance to practice and develop their own scholarly style.

More often than not the seminar paper's purpose was left ambiguous in written instructions (which were typically a few sentences in a syllabus, if there were any at all) or in class discussions. Students were left to figure out purposes and intended audiences for themselves.

When asked what confuses her about seminar papers, one participant reflected:

> I think it's what my professor wants. No, back up. It's who the paper is for and what the paper is supposed to be accomplishing is really what it comes down to. So, I've had professors who were, like, "This paper should be aimed to be an article when we're done. Right? That's what we're aiming for." So, he has you choose a journal that you're going to submit it to, and you tell him that, and so, he's reading it in mind of that journal and whether it's going to be good for that journal in ways that you can change if you were to send it to another journal or whatever. And so, that's helpful, right? But then there are professors who don't seem to want that as a goal. And I'm confused by that constantly.

Another said, "The boundaries can be so nebulous. I have to define it for myself, right? If I don't, it will be even more massively anxiety-producing than it normally is."

While writing to learn frequently conflicted with professionalization, grading was humming in the background (and grades might play an even bigger role in terminal MA programs, where students may not be looking to the longer horizon of a research-intensive faculty career). Most of our interviewees were squeamish about discussing grades, though less so with Gabriel, a fellow doctoral student who conducted most of the interviews, than with Tom, the faculty member who conducted fewer. One remarked that grades are

> kind of looming there. You know that it is something that's going to be graded. ... So, it is something that's there, but it also doesn't get a lot of airtime in class. ... And so, it's just kind of something that's assumed that you know is coming.

One participant from Taiwan, the only international student among our interviewees, put teacher assessment in the foreground, acknowledging the default and dominant "teacher as evaluator" rhetorical situation that prevails for nearly all school writing:

> We write seminar papers because professors want to assess our learning and figure out what knowledge we have retained or need to expand and improve. Writing seminar papers becomes a chance for us students to show professors that we have paid attention and learned what they want us to take away. A seminar paper, in my mind, should have three features: a specific topic, a clear theoretical framework, and clear, concise writing.

A final and rather unexpected purpose—one discussed in detail in the next section—concerns how writing seminar papers is often a means of mediating and managing relationships with faculty.

Confusion about purpose is amplified by the fact that the graduate students in our study seemed to *want* the seminar paper to be a chance to explore something they were passionate about. However, they often disclosed this obliquely in statements tinged with uncertainty, embarrassment, or contradictions. They seemed torn between the intrinsic desire to pursue something exciting to them and the extrinsic pressure for the writing to please their professors, earn a good grade, and develop into a publishable artifact that would help them secure a job in a tough market.

Competing and even contradictory purposes are familiar to genre theorists who study writing and discourse. Rhetorical genre theory frames genres not merely as a set of formal features but as *tools* for use. Genres are "ways of recognizing, responding to, acting meaningfully and consequentially within, and helping to reproduce recurrent situations" (Bawarshi and Reiff 2010, 3). They are a mode of *social action* (Miller 1984).

This approach calls attention to purpose, to what the genre does in a community rather than what it looks like; it further analyzes how writers selectively understand and use the tools at their disposal. Understood this way, the seminar paper is a genre that performs certain kinds of reasonably predictable actions; it is a tool that faculty and graduate students inherit and "take up" (Freadman 2002). But that does not mean that the genre's purpose is singular or its uptake consistent. The same genre can be deployed in a community of practice in service of multiple motives, but this usually introduces double binds or contradictions that can compromise the genre's ability to successfully perform effective social action (Lundell and Beach 2003; Freadman and Adam 1996). Systems can ignore contradictions, but not without some cost; in this case, graduate students pay the cost in uncertainty and frustration.

Still, participants in our study were eloquent in analyzing their own circumstances, developing pragmatic strategies for balancing ambiguous objectives, and coming up with creative proposals related to how the seminar paper genre could be more aligned with their individual goals at a given stage in their graduate careers (e.g., a class presentation, a digital initiative, a public humanities project, an exploration of how to teach course material in other contexts, and a literature review).

> I think as the expectation shifts from it being just, you know, to fulfill a class but instead to advance your individual career and to give you things that you can work with. . . . Grades really don't matter, and at this point, it's kind of on the students themselves, like if they're doing all the work and staying engaged with the class. So, if our purpose or goal is really to develop graduate students into scholars, it should be more individually driven and less like school, if that makes sense.

That kind of individualized approach is rare, and, as a consequence, participants in this study paid an emotional cost in anxiety, stress, and uncertainty as they shuttled among multiple objectives within the constraints of one genre.

Writing at the graduate level is deeply linked to students' identities, aspirations, and sense of self-efficacy (Ivanič 1998; Prior 1998; Curry 2016). Trying (and often failing) to meet multiple demands simultaneously results in feelings of inadequacy or shame. Participants in our study often described feeling reluctant to turn in papers that they felt had missed the mark on several levels. Some even went so far as to say that the experience was stressful to the point of being unproductive:

> [I]f I write a crappy paper in the last week of class, like sure I should go back to it and revise it and make it not crappy, but it's like a traumatic experience now, and I don't even want to think about it.

There is no easy solution to the questions of purpose raised in this section, but faculty and graduate program directors should raise such questions explicitly and negotiate them out in the open.

PEOPLE: "I THINK IT'S A CHANCE FOR YOU TO GET TO TALK WITH THIS PROFESSOR"

This section is properly an extension of the one above on *purpose*, but we opted to set it apart because of its complexity and salience. The greatest surprise of our interviewing was that in addition to learning, professionalization, and grades, a fourth motive emerged: seminar papers are a means of creating, maintaining, and managing relationships with faculty. One participant stated this candidly when she wrote her definition of the seminar paper:

> A seminar paper should be the opportunity try new ideas/methods/writing about new texts with a professor you may want to keep working with in the future. . . . It should also be about building a good working relationship with your professor.

Our informants helped us appreciate how *interpersonal* this process is for doctoral students and how much relational concerns weigh on them as they compose. We concluded that the seminar paper genre is, part of a social strategy for managing short- and long-term relationships in graduate school.

When asked about the purpose of a seminar paper, the first thing one interviewee said was, "I think it's a chance for you to get to talk with this professor. Like this professor is giving you their time." Another participant, referring to his advisor, told us that the seminar paper is "this, like, dialogue between us." On its surface, a twenty-page paper in rough manuscript form might seem inanimate, impersonal, and perhaps even lonely—associated as it often is with long hours spent writing in solitude. However, throughout our interviews, students in our study saw it as deeply social. Even when there was no direct conversation between student and professor, they characterized the textual transactions—the exchange of their writing and the comments on the papers returned by their professors—as meaningful interactions with *people*, not merely texts or ideas.

These student-professor interactions were often fraught with anxiety, even as participants described how valuable they were. One participant confessed:

> I have a pretty open relationship with my advisor, but there's still, like, a subconscious thing: I think that we don't want our advisors or potential committee members to, like, realize that we aren't smart enough or something, that we should already be on that level. Even though the whole point is to get us to that level, right?

Although it's tempting to think of the seminar paper genre as a dispassionate intellectual exercise, participants in our study revealed that the socio-emotional motives driving the genre—fear, shame, longing for approval, excitement about mutual intellectual engagement—were more important and viscerally immediate than the motives of learning, professionalization, and grades discussed in the previous section of this chapter.

These emotional responses make sense when one considers the high-stakes negotiations that the seminar paper genre invisibly mediates. "[W]hen you're in coursework, you don't have a committee and people who have—I mean, you have your advisor—but people who you can just, like, use their time to help you with their stuff," one of our participants told us. "So, I think that's part of it. Like trying out working with people." For graduate students, the approval of professors doesn't feel like a superficial or short-term experience. Maintaining good status with academic advisors is often crucial to securing the professional opportunities and academic sponsorship (e.g., dissertation readers, letters of recommendation, and coauthored articles) that graduate students rely on to achieve professional success (Poe et al. 2010). In a way, the seminar paper is a chance for graduate students to persuade professors of their value in ways that go well beyond the grade the paper will earn.

Relationships with peers and other academics in the field came up in our conversations with participants, but not as often; the student-professor relationship tended to take precedence. This may be due to the professor's role as grade-giver, a relationship that has been reinforced through years of prior schooling. It also seems likely that graduate students in coursework see building strong relationships with faculty as a crucial step to eventually developing relationships with other academics in their fields.

In sum, our interviews revealed how central the seminar paper genre was to building, managing, and maintaining relationships with faculty in graduate school. This feature may be unique to graduate education, given how entangled professional development is with personal relationships.

PROCESS

Seminars in literary studies naturally focus on reading. The degree to which faculty attend to writing—beyond assigning a paper—varies enormously. Our interviewees described some professors who scheduled in a sequence of proposals, literature reviews, abstracts, and drafts to scaffold a final essay; some who required a mid-semester paper as an opportunity to test an idea or method; some who included peer review; some who scheduled presentations on emerging seminar papers toward the end of the semester; some who invited students to meet in conferences; and some who did none of these things. Participants in our study deeply appreciated faculty who included deliberate, iterative, and interactive writing stages paced throughout the semester. "I generally interact with a lot of writing anxiety," said one, echoing the sentiment of many, "so the more guidance I have, the better."

One professor's courses—the one mentioned above in the Purpose section—proved especially influential. Everyone in our interview cohort who had taken one or more of his seminars commented, without our prompting, on the value of his rigorous, example-rich, interactive writing assignments that built incrementally toward an end-of-term paper: two different-sized abstracts, a proposal, a first five pages, a bibliography, and a peer-review session. Some cited this as the *only* time in their graduate coursework when they were forced to start early and participate in an extended writing process.

This professor framed publication as the dominant goal (and indeed this seminar seems to generate more publication success than others), but students appreciated his process independent of that purpose. We got the impression that even if he had switched his allegiance to more exploratory, writing-to-learn priorities, students would still have preferred his approach to teaching invention and composing. And it was not just that he segmented the writing process into stages but also that he shared *student* examples at each stage and discussed them in class. One participant who had never taken this professor's seminars also echoed the utility of student samples:

> I think one of the challenges of seminar papers is that we don't read other people's seminar papers, right? So, I don't know if what I'm doing is normal. Like, I have no idea. I know what a published article looks like, but I would assume they look very different from graduate student seminar papers.

Written instructions are no substitute for a process-rich pedagogy. Our participants noted that instructions were often provided in a paragraph or two on the syllabus, but they found those of little use. Conversations with faculty and peers proved considerably more helpful. We heard several stories of faculty formally or informally holding individual conferences that shifted or sharpened the participant's understanding of the seminar paper genre (and often their confidence too). Written feedback on a mid-semester paper can similarly shape expectations, some reported, but this of course applies only *if* such an earlier paper is assigned.

More often than not, as one participant remarked, "There's not a ton of direction. . . . They essentially say, 'Write a seminar paper. It should be 20 pages.'" Many professors even sideline writing at the very end of the semester by assigning major reading right through the final class. Most in our cohort seemed resigned to a curriculum in literary studies that treats composing and revising as—to borrow Doreen Starke-Meyerring's analysis of how most disciplines quietly evade writing pedagogy at the graduate level—"normalized, transparent, invisible, . . . rendering writing a non-question" (92). We expect students to perform disciplinary genres on demand, in short order, in relative isolation, which in turn provokes considerable uncertainty and anxiety, even shame.

Anxiety is also driven by the press of time, which emerged as a persistent theme:

> It's time. It's the reading load and teaching, and it's picking between grading or doing well on this draft, and it's just not—it's not a fun position to be in. And I know that I can do better things than what's coming out. . . . It's not that I don't want to do it or that I don't enjoy it, because I do enjoy doing this.

Another reflected, "We [as graduate instructors] tell our students not to cram the night before, but how many of us are doing that thing?" Time constraints likewise stoke skepticism about learning and professional outcomes, particularly when paired with the contradictions of purpose discussed earlier:

> I don't know if I would ask for, like, some beautiful article at the end of the semester because I don't think it's realistic given how many classes you're in and what you're doing. . . . It gets really frustrating because it feels like I just don't have the time to create the thing that they want me to create. . . . [T]here's a clear disconnect between the reality of how many things we have going on and how much time we have to put into this.

PEDAGOGICAL IMPLICATIONS

The above sections attempt to capture the lived experience of graduate students. What follows is a return to the highlighted themes and a discussion of pragmatic recommendations for faculty who play a role in running graduate programs.

Purpose: Don't make the seminar paper do too many things—and be more explicit about its purpose. Graduate students tend to be highly motivated and capable of clearly defining goals for their writing; they were, after all, admitted to a selective academic program. But they're not immune to the confusion that comes with acculturating to a specialized academic community, especially when the purposes of their writing are ambiguous or numerous. One student paper is unlikely to be both a write-to-learn activity that allows students to explore new (to them) material *and* a draft of a professional publication. A professional scholar doesn't start a research project in a new field and churn out an article in a couple of months. It isn't realistic to expect novices to do this either. Seminars may need to choose a dominant motive and should make this explicit to avoid the ambiguity and anxiety reported by participants in our study.

Of course, seminars often include a diverse range of students. Some may be MA students encountering the material for the first time, while others may be PhD students who already have a good grasp of the field. In addition to having metacognitive discussions about seminar paper motives and purposes, faculty might consider allowing students to define and choose their own goals for their papers. One of our study's participants said, "I think our final project should be useful in some way," but defined "usefulness" by referring to a range of possibilities: pedagogical applications, future publications, or simply a better understanding of a new area of the field. Programs should likewise have this conversation about purpose.

This does not mean homogenizing the seminar paper to fulfill one purpose across a program; after all, graduate programs serve multiple purposes, and individuals within those programs have varying goals and motives—individual students will even cycle through different motives depending on timing (beginning students have different goals than they will as dissertators, for example). What is important is acknowledging the variation that exists in the program and creating a curriculum that meets the needs of a diverse population. This could involve designing some seminars for professionalization and others for learning, creating different final project options within seminars for students based on their goals, or developing separate "tracks" for students within programs. The most critical thing—at either the seminar or program level—is to acknowledge that one genre can't do everything, and to be transparent about this with students.

People: Create more opportunities for in-person and intertextual (drafts and feedback) interaction. The solution to student confusion about the seminar paper is probably *not* to write longer, more detailed assignment sheets or even to provide students with a handbook about writing seminar papers. Instead, invest more time in faculty interactions, especially outside of class.

Our study revealed how much personal encounters matter in shaping genre expectations. Mentorly interactions with faculty in offices, hallways, and classrooms not only helped students to compose more sophisticated papers and take more risks but also registered effects far beyond the bounds of a single project. These interactions, which Margaret Price (2011) has described as taking place within *kairotic spaces*, can and should take a variety of forms, acknowledging diversity of students and contexts. In our study, even conversations of a few minutes proved formative to how students conceptualized graduate writing.

Process: Design each course to include an early, iterative, interactive writing process. Patricia Sullivan (1991) called for addressing the composition process in graduate seminars nearly thirty years ago, and an increasing number of other voices have echoed her call (Rose and McClafferty 2001;

Micciche and Carr 2011; Simpson et al. 2016). A process approach is the consensus best practice at earlier grade levels ("Framework" 2011; "WPA" 2014), but graduate faculty too often implicitly or explicitly presume graduate writing somehow works differently, that graduate students should be able to perform the seminar essay genre on demand and manage the writing process on their own. Building progressive writing sequences into a seminar does not compromise rigor—in fact, most of our participants reported that their most demanding and productive seminars were ones that included an extended, scaffolded writing regimen.

Setting early or optional deadlines, however, is not enough. There need to be occasions, including class time, to *work* on writing. Participants in our study likewise valued opportunities for peer review, conferences with faculty, presentations on projects in progress, and other chances to share and revise their work throughout the semester. Also important is weaving authentic *student* examples of seminar papers—not just published articles—into such activities and having meta-discussions about them in class.

Programs could even maintain an archive of student papers, keyed to different purposes. Still, none of these recommendations will do any good if students don't have time to focus on their writing well before the semester ends. Layering in more writing work for students without carving out time for them to get this work done—by tapering down the reading, for example, during weeks when drafts are due—will create even more double binds for students already juggling complex academic and life demands.

We have provided these recommendations on the premise that the seminar paper must be assigned, but following the themes we have been investigating to their logical conclusion provokes more basic questions: Does the traditional seminar paper need to be assigned at all, in every course? Are there better ways for graduate students to learn and professionalize? As one participant reflected, "It seems like some of them you just write them, and then they, like—you never think about it again, and then they just kind of go somewhere to die." Another remarked on how graduate programs might achieve better results if they create space for students to be more strategic and intentional in choosing course projects, including options distant from the seminar paper genre:

> I don't think we should have to write a seminar paper for every class. . . . In cases where graduate students are taking three classes. . . . I think it would be

most productive to just let them pick one of those classes to write a seminar paper on and then for the other ones maybe do something else like an in-class presentation . . . because we could write so much better seminar papers if we had to do only one instead of three at the same time. And then I think the rate of seminar papers that end up becoming articles or dissertation chapters would be so much higher because each one would be like we actually care about it and have the time to dedicate to it and not force it out.

Part II

ARGUMENT, ETHOS, AND INTERVENTION

Chapter 3

The Seminar Essay as Academic Literary Criticism

Strategies for Entering the Scholarly Conversation

Almas Khan

> *Language is not a neutral medium that passes freely and easily into the private property of the speaker's intentions; it is populated—overpopulated—with the intentions of others. Expropriating it, forcing it to submit to one's own intentions and accents, is a difficult and complicated process.*
>
> Mikhail Bakhtin, "Discourse in the Novel" (1992, 294)

In *The Dialogic Imagination*, Mikhail Bakhtin theorized that the novel's multi-vocality posed creative and critical challenges, but also opportunities to showcase linguistic mastery. It follows that graduate students in literary studies may experience anxiety alongside excitement about embarking on their first seminar essays. Seminar essays generically resemble journal articles: they typically span fifteen to thirty double-spaced pages and are distinguished from much undergraduate writing by their ostensible originality and depth of research.

While the seminar essay as a genre has come under critique (Hayot 2014, 9–12), seminar essays ideally refine students' analytical abilities and enable students to develop a distinctive authorial voice as they converse with other members of a scholarly community. Learning how to dialogue effectively with fellow scholars in a field is vital; as two journal editors assert, "We can't overstate how important this element is: it is the one thing from which everything else—in both abstract and essay—flows" (Halpern and Phelan 2017). Numerous textbooks, handbooks, and other scholarly works (notably in composition studies and linguistics) have discussed how university students at different stages can intervene cogently in critical conversations. Targeting undergraduates, Graff and Birkenstein (2018) provide advice on situating "moves" in literary criticism. Irene Clark (2006), meanwhile, provides general guidance for graduates on their capstone projects.

In its sophistication, the graduate seminar essay is usually a hybrid of an undergraduate research paper and a master's thesis or PhD dissertation chapter. Additionally, the seminar essay's generic kinship with journal articles suggests ambitions beyond fulfilling course requirements, namely, participating publicly in a scholarly dialogue. Drawing upon research on academic writing in general and contemporary debates about literary criticism's value in particular, this chapter will demonstrate how students composing seminar essays can skillfully join a scholarly conversation and thus become recognized members of an academic community.

The initial section will define what literary criticism is and analyze the seminar essay as a special, intermediary genre of literary criticism. Next, this chapter will parse the metaphor of a scholarly conversation and conceptualize how to intervene in the conversation at different levels and in a range of affirmative to defensive ways. Tips for overcoming challenges in engaging with prior scholarship will also be presented. A closing section will dissect critical conversation moves in two published articles, noting substantive and stylistic techniques. By envisioning the seminar essay through a writing-as-social-practice lens, this chapter will underscore the empowering capacities of literary criticism, which at its finest can constitute literature itself (see Brodkey 1987 and Wilde 1982).

THE SEMINAR ESSAY'S PURPOSES AS ACADEMIC LITERARY CRITICISM

Current writing about literature, whether in more public-facing forms like book reviews or more academic forms like scholarly monographs, is predominantly in the critical mode. Criticism encompasses "[t]he art of estimating the qualities and character of literary or artistic work" (*OED Online*), and Western literary criticism's origins date to the ancient Greeks (Blamires 1991, 1). Today, though, the term "criticism" has more specific connotations for literary scholars, namely, using the "hermeneutics of suspicion"[1] to probe the surface of texts and uncover new meanings.

Theoretical frameworks through which texts may be decoded include formalism, psychoanalysis, Marxism, feminism, reader-response criticism, deconstruction, new historicism, postcolonialism, critical race studies, and ecocriticism.[2] However, citing the infirmities of established approaches, scholars have recently advocated a postcritical turn to alternative modes of analysis such as affective readings (Anker and Felski 2017, 10), thereby expanding the toolkit available to seminar essay writers. Students must paradoxically use this extensive research to advance new claims, paralleling the challenge T. S. Eliot's essay "Tradition and the Individual Talent" (1919) identified for poets.

The seminar essay shares attributes with literature and with other forms of literary criticism, but it emerges from the unique rhetorical context of graduate academia. The primary audience for the essay is a professor who is likely an expert in the field, and the essay's immediate purpose is to prove the writer's command of course material. The essay ordinarily uses course texts and discussions as a springboard to deep dive into an under-researched issue. For instance, a syllabus from one of the author's graduate seminars advised students that their "papers should, in one fashion or another, illuminate one of the broad topics we are exploring" (Ramazani 2012). The criteria for evaluating papers' efficacy were "original and sustained argument, rigorous and subtle critical analysis, theoretical reach, and sophisticated use of evidence and secondary research" (Ramazani 2012). Similar criteria often apply to higher-order graduate documents.

Strategically, then, in composing a given seminar essay, students may endeavor to reflect on the course but also lay the groundwork for their next projects. While seminar essays are an important means for students to discover new scholarly fields, producing a corpus of essays in a specific field can strengthen students' fluency with key dialogue partners, thus easing the process of writing a thesis or dissertation. Seminar essays may additionally be revised into publishable articles; for motivation, students may even view the essays not as rote class assignments but as article drafts (Semenza 2010, 91–92), keeping in mind that academic journal articles have a diffuser audience than seminar essays. As prestigious article placements are imperative for students aspiring to obtain research-based academic positions, the seminar essay's importance has become magnified.

Less instrumentally and more inspirationally, the seminar essay's raison d'être mirrors that of the literature it elucidates. Samuel Johnson argued that literature's main functions were to instruct and delight (Johnson 1778); a seminar essay analogously teaches readers about literary texts and, ideally, resonates emotionally. Mario Vargas Llosa has enthused about how literary criticism captivated his consciousness as a student:

> In these luminous pages, thinking, imagining and inventing through writing were shown to be a magnificent way to act and make one's mark on history. Every chapter made it clear that great social upheavals or small individual destinies were expressed in visceral form in the impalpable world of ideas and literary fiction. (Vargas Llosa 2015, 88)

Among other purposes, literary criticism may seek to instigate social and political changes (Pfister 2000); more privately, it can be a form of autobiography, as the author illuminates the self through analyzing literary texts (Freedman et al. 1993). These transcendent aims can inspire memorable seminar essays, which balance creativity with an attunement to discursive conventions, such as participating appropriately in the critical conversation.

INTERVENING IN THE SCHOLARLY CONVERSATION: THEORY AND PRACTICE

The conversational metaphor for academic writing is frequently credited to Kenneth Burke, who transposed an intellectual task into a more tangible register by inviting readers to:

> Imagine that you enter a parlor. You come late. When you arrive, others have long preceded you, and they are engaged in a heated discussion, a discussion too heated for them to pause and tell you exactly what it is about. In fact, the discussion had already begun long before any of them got there, so that no one present is qualified to retrace for you all the steps that had gone before. You listen for a while, until you decide that you have caught the tenor of the argument; then you put in your oar. Someone answers, you answer him; another comes to

your defense; another aligns himself against you, to either the embarrassment or gratification of your opponent, depending upon the quality of your ally's assistance. However, the discussion is interminable. The hour grows late, you must depart. And you do depart, with the discussion still vigorously in progress. (Burke 1973, 110–11)

The parlor discussion metaphor here encapsulates three significant features of academic writing: its relative formality, grounding in research, and emphasis on persuasive argumentation. A parlor (or contemporary living room) is a space for formal discourse, much like an academic journal.

In noting that readers enter the parlor in medias res, the passage references their not necessarily understanding how the conversation in the parlor has progressed thus far. In a physical parlor, a polite guest would become acquainted with the nature of the dialogue before talking; academic writers must similarly know the state of the scholarly conversation before interjecting. Just as parties to a parlor debate stake out positions, academic writers must have contestable theses. Ultimately, though, no piece of scholarship is likely to be the final word on a disputed issue, serving instead as a catalyst for further discussion that repeats the process described above.

Burke emphasizes that academic writers must reconstruct the relevant critical conversation before writing, as knowing what other scholars have said on a topic clarifies the author's original contribution to the field. Graduate students may find it beneficial to conceptualize different levels at which critical conversations can occur in literary studies, as well as varying types of interventions that they may make. Critical conversations can range from the more local to the more global levels, as suggested by the following four-category schematic:

(1) *Conversations about a specific text or texts, or a particular author's oeuvre*: the standard seminar essay in literary studies close reads one or more texts to offer a new interpretation of the work(s). Students may focus on a single text or compare and contrast multiple texts. Research here entails determining how other scholars have construed the text(s), and the essay dialogues with their interpretations.

Extending up a level, and generally requiring more research, essays may intervene in conversations about an author's oeuvre. In major author classes, where students are likely to have read a substantial body of work by one or more authors, analysis at this level may be mandatory.

(2) *Conversations about a literary movement, genre, theory, or other field*: moving beyond dialogue about specific texts and authors, scholars may converse about literary movements (e.g., Anglo-American modernism), genres (e.g., poetry), and theories (e.g., poststructuralism). Other types of fields may be defined by, inter alia, time period or identity characteristics such as nationality, race and ethnicity, and gender and sexuality. Illustrative examples include Renaissance literature, American literature, black diasporic literature, and queer literature.

Wide knowledge of a field, beyond a few texts, is essential to contribute meaningfully to critical conversations at this level. While students cannot be expected to master new fields in a semester, class materials can orient students within the field, allowing them to intervene in a fairly specific conversation even as they retain a broader perspective. In addition, students may be familiar with the field from earlier classes, and materials from those courses may facilitate the essay-writing process.

(3) *Meta-conversations, as on translation, the nature of literature, or the discipline of literary studies*: meta-conversations about literature and literary studies have burgeoned as of late; in the United States, this development may result partially from declining enrollment in literature programs and public wariness about higher education more generally (Flaherty 2018 and Marken 2019). A heightened sense of crisis pervades current meta-conversations, but literary critics in earlier eras were preoccupied with similar questions about the value of literature and literary criticism.

Seminar essays can be a space to ponder these philosophical issues, either at a relatively abstract level or more concretely while dissecting texts. Essays involving meta-conversations can prompt students to reflect on why they are pursuing advanced degrees and how they see their career unfolding in light of present conditions.

(4) *Interdisciplinary conversations*: paeans to interdisciplinarity abound in literature departments today, and literary scholars increasingly rely on methodologies and ideas from other disciplines to reshape understandings of literary texts. Trending interdisciplinary approaches include literature, science, and technology (e.g., environmental literature and the digital humanities); literature and art; and law and literature.

Many literary scholars have formal training in a second discipline, but others hone skills more informally while researching and teaching.

Acquiring proficiency in a second discipline enables scholars to intervene in conversations beyond those in literary studies, potentially enlarging readership for their work. Most seminar professors are amenable to interdisciplinarity, with the caveat that essays should be grounded in literary studies. Students must walk a disciplinary tightrope in their essays, however, as superficial engagement with the other discipline may also be frowned upon.

The title of a particular course, as well as the specific topics covered, can cue students to which conversations they must or may participate in. The research universe will thus shrink, and it will contract further based on students' interests and expertise. Hence time constraints dictate that students concentrate on reviewing scholarship that is most pertinent to their essay's thesis.

While scrutinizing this work, students should decide upon the type of intervention their essays will make vis-à-vis existing research: affirmative, defensive, or mixed. In brief, "Are you intervening by saying 'yes and,' 'yes but,' 'no' or some combination of those responses?" (Phelan and Halpern 2018). These varying relationships with other scholars' writings can be conceived as follows:

(1) *"Yes and" interventions*: scholarship that affirms claims in prior conversations, but aims to add a new point to the dialogue, can be classified as a "yes and" intervention. Gap-filling essays are a popular form of supplemental intervention; authors acknowledge earlier related scholarship but seek to fill a hole in the research. Writers must nevertheless justify why the scholarly lacuna they have identified is worth filling, as not every issue untreated in the scholarship merits research.

(2) *"Yes but" interventions*: scholarship that agrees with the gist of a conversation, but undertakes to qualify or nuance previous claims, can be seen as a "yes but" intervention. The balanced approach of such an intervention reflects agreement and disagreement with earlier research. Academia's love of subtlety results in this means of intervention being common. One possible pitfall, though, is that writers may fail to take a clear position on an issue, frustrating some readers.

(3) *"No" interventions*: the liveliest type of scholarship may be the "no" intervention, in which a piece fundamentally disagrees with other researchers' claims. Essays challenging prevalent wisdom in a field, including interpretations of a text, represent a classic mode of negative

intervention. However, just as parlor conversations should be civil, authors should refrain from distortion and ad hominem attacks. Scholarly fields are cliquish, and breaches of etiquette can have reputational repercussions.

A thesis statement must succinctly capture what critical conversation(s) the essay is intervening in and what the nature of the essay's intervention is. Finding equilibrium between prior scholarship and one's original argument in the thesis, and later in the essay's main body, can be an arduous process. This problem may nonetheless be mitigated through an awareness of how to troubleshoot issues that often arise when negotiating between others' voices and one's own.

During the research stage, a "literature review" of extant research is crucial to glean lines of conversation and to ensure that the essay has not been preempted. Tasks in the research phase include finding, organizing, and interpreting scholarship. General and field-specific research guides are available (see, for example, Brookbank and Christenberry 2019 and Mattiuozzi and Lindsay 2008), and the *MLA International Bibliography* is a frequent starting point.

Consulting the seminar professor and librarians, particularly those specializing in literary studies or the essay's field(s) more specifically, can be helpful as well. While researching can be incessant, once a set of sources is talking in a closed circuit—that is, the authors are citing one another—it is likely that the major scholarship has been located. As a shortcut, students may find the most relevant, reputable, and recent source on the essay's topic and examine how that source defines key terms and portrays the current state of the scholarly dialogue.[3] Keeping track of a voluminous amount of research is an additional challenge, but a research log can be valuable (Ballenger 2017, 102–4). Lastly, research may be facilitated if students adopt critical reading practices (Wallace and Wray 2016), such as taking notes in a journal and creating visual aids.

Students are inclined to linger in the research or listening phase of the composition process and delay transitioning to the writing or speaking phase. However, they should begin drafting their essay as soon as they are confident that they could contribute substantially to the conversation if they were in a room with leading scholars on the subject (Kibbe 2016, 78–79). Should supplemental research then become necessary, students can research more productively on specific issues rather than feeling inundated by a tidal wave of scholarship.

Having to build on this prior work and present an argument of one's own can cause substantive, linguistic, and citational problems; fortunately, remedies also exist. Regarding substance, essays may synthesize current scholarship elegantly but not say anything new on a subject. Such literature review essays are sometimes acceptable, as in essays intended to feed into a larger project, but in general professors commend originality. The conversational metaphor can address this concern: as a thought experiment, how would one respond to an interlocutor who asked about the essay's central new insight?

A related linguistic problem comes from overlarding the essay with disciplinary jargon as a substitute for true analysis. This phenomenon may be attributed to the steep learning curve for a new field and the "imposter syndrome" afflicting many graduate students (Blake-Hedges 2019). Some jargon is vital in literary criticism, but students should cast any sentences with needless jargon into their own words.

Lastly, while not being too deferential to other scholars, students should be meticulous about acknowledging their conversation partners in citations. Much as students in seminars ideally recognize classmates whose comments inspire their oral remarks, they should credit textual dialogue partners.[4] Although some plagiarism is deliberate, more frequently students mistake source language for their own, a problem that can be rectified by making thorough research notes and allocating ample time for revision. Understanding these pragmatic challenges and the theoretical dimensions of entering a scholarly conversation allows students to craft essays that may have rhetorical affinities with the published articles evaluated next.

SCHOLARLY DIALOGUE: ILLUSTRATIVE CLOSE READINGS AND CLOSING THOUGHTS

Studying articles in a given seminar essay's field(s) can acculturate students to discursive conventions; one professor recommends that students spend at least two hours per week reviewing current articles in their fields' top journals (Semenza 2010, 92–93). While reading, students should concentrate not just on the gist of the argument but on how claims are presented, documenting any useful strategies. This analytical process is modeled below through parsing substantively and stylistically disparate introductions to articles in major journals of American and world literature.

The first example article is from *American Literature*, and it epitomizes what many seminar essays do in creatively applying an established theoretical paradigm to a specific literary text. The article, Kate McCullough's, "'The Complexity of Loss Itself': The Comics Form and *Fun Home*'s Queer Reparative Temporality" assesses Alison Bechdel's 2006 graphic memoir *Fun Home: A Family Tragicomic* from a queer theory perspective. In the following thesis paragraph, McCullough explains the article's intervention in the critical conversation:

> While scholars have productively assessed both the recursive structure of *Fun Home*'s narrative and the thematics of the archive in it, I will focus here on the interplay of form and story, the ways in which the temporal openings inherent in the comic form itself make possible a queer recasting of time. By deploying the temporal openings of the graphic form, *Fun Home* challenges the putative fixity of heteronormative family time and the temporality of kinship lines more broadly. Bechdel represents this queering of generation and kinship as a constituent part of the young Alison's coming-of-age as a comics artist; this temporal reworking simultaneously makes possible a reparative web of affiliation. I see the graphic form itself as the crucial condition for the text's production of a reparative reading of that past: ultimately, the story Bechdel tells of both her father's and her own sexuality relies on the comics form to produce a queerly ambivalent yet healing account of Alison's life and her father's suicide. (McCullough 2018, 378–79, citation omitted)

The article's subtitle, "The Comics Form and *Fun Home*'s Queer Reparative Temporality," indicates that the interplay between form and time in *Fun Home* will be at the argument's core. The preceding passage thus elaborates on how attentiveness to the graphic form of *Fun Home*, and especially modes of representing time within the form, can enhance understandings of the memoir.

McCullough frames this intervention as a "yes and" type, citing earlier *Fun Home* scholarship ("scholars have productively assessed . . .") but indicating a new direction for the article ("I will focus here . . ."). This sentence also alludes to key terms in queer studies, that is, the archive and recursivity.

McCullough particularly asserts that the graphic form of *Fun Home* challenges conventional views of time, and that a queer perception of the past helps Alison to heal from a traumatic upbringing. Such a text-specific level of intervening in the critical conversation is standard for seminar essays, but loftier interventions may be expected as well.

For instance, McCullough's introduction signals the article's engagement with higher-level conversations about form, queer theory, and critical reading. This dialogic expansiveness is evident from the article's outset; the epigraph quotes an influential article by Eve Kosofsky Sedgwick on paranoid reading and reparative reading (McCullough 2018, 377, quoting Sedgwick 1997). Later, McCullough posits that "Bechdel's reparative stance might also be taken as hailing queer theory's attention, reminding us of the queer potentiality of the comics form itself," especially given the form's ability to depict the complexity of memory (McCullough 2018, 379).

McCullough ends the article's introduction by arguing that Bechdel's memoir exemplifies "how to read comics queerly" (McCullough 2018, 381), flagging the article's utility for readers curious about how to interpret graphic texts in general. Form- and theory-intensive seminars may require that essays intervene in conversations beyond those involving a specific text, and McCullough's article demonstrates one approach. Overall, the introduction highlights how interpretive ingenuity can coexist with a deep commitment to the critical conversation.

Perusing articles in prominent journals reveals a variety of effective means to intervene in the critical conversation; no one formula fits every writer and context. Seminar essays can therefore be an opportunity for students to experiment with intervention styles. For example, a recent article in *Modern Philology* employs different rhetorical strategies than McCullough's article while construing obscure historical texts from a relatively defensive posture.

The article, Emily Weissbourd's "Translating Spain: Purity of Blood and Orientalism in Mabbe's *Rogue* and *Guzmán de Alfarache*," starts with a contextualized close reading of the two main literary texts to be evaluated, Mateo Alemán's picaresque novel *Guzmán de Alfarache* (1599, 1604) and, the first English translation of the novel, James Mabbe's *The Rogue* (1622) (Weissbourd 2017, 552–53, citing Alemán 2001 and Alemán 1967). In contrast, McCullough's article began with an epigraph from a renowned scholar, a form of instant immersion in the critical conversation. As the novelty of Weissbourd's article derives from its analyzing literary texts not widely known in the field, Weissbourd leads with the primary works to entice readers.

After acquainting readers with the texts, the introduction pivots to a roadmap paragraph summarizing each section of the article and the article's contribution to the critical conversation. This paragraph, excerpted in part below, affirms the article's scholarly significance:

> I have divided the essay into three sections. The first lays out the stakes of this project and its broader implications for the field. I explain why the study of a now largely unread picaresque novel can inform scholarship on more widely studied early modern English literature like the plays of Marlowe and Shakespeare. In order to do so, I discuss some outstanding questions that have been raised by twentieth- and twenty-first-century scholarship that foregrounds the importance of Spain to discourses of race in early modern England. I then describe the historical context that surrounds *Guzmán* as well as its publication history in the seventeenth century in order to demonstrate why this particular translation speaks to those outstanding questions. (Weissbourd 2017, 553)

Although the article's primary intervention is in the field of early modern English literature, Weissbourd is also in dialogue with historians who study emerging European discourses of race; the first footnote in the article's main body catalogues historical scholarship on race (Weissbourd 2017, 554). Discreetly suggesting that the article constitutes a mild "no" or strong "yes but" intervention in these literary and historical critical conversations, Weissbourd later in the introduction argues that scrutinizing the linguistic differences between *Guzmán de Alfarache* and *The Rogue* could "destabilize Spain's status as a presumed site of origin for discourses of race in the period" (Weissbourd 2017, 554).

The article's next section presents the field's consensus position, which is then challenged through a comparative close reading. The roadmap paragraph here also implicitly responds to critics skeptical of the article's importance by explaining how the interpretation of arcane works can revolutionize scholarship on canonical English literature of the period, such as plays by Christopher Marlowe and William Shakespeare. Taking a minority stance in the field's critical conversation and having to justify a focus on so-called minor texts can require rhetorical gymnastics, but bolder arguments are more likely to result in transformative scholarship.

The seminar essay enables students to develop the academic literacy necessary for becoming pioneers in their fields. As part of the disciplinary acclimatization process, students confront a self-community dialectic that may be evocative of similar tensions in the literature they interpret and in their lives outside academia. Assuming academic writing "is an act of identity" (Hyland 2002), the seminar essay is a crucible in which students' identities are forged. Through mastering the difficult art of conversing with other scholars, students become integrated into an academic community. Their scholarly work can more broadly enrich conversations beyond academia by sparking public appreciation of literature's power to illuminate and re-envision human experience. Academic literary criticism, which at its best is a dialogic and imaginative form, ultimately can remake understandings of literary texts as a way of remaking the world.

NOTES

1. Paul Ricoeur (1970) distinguished between a "school of suspicion" and an interpretive school seeking the "restoration of meaning."

2. For an overview of these theoretical approaches, see Dobie 2012.

3. However, just as students should read primary literary texts rather than rely exclusively on others' interpretations, reading key scholarship cited in a piece is imperative.

4. Students should be especially mindful not to reproduce inequities in the discipline through exclusionary citation practices (Delgado 1992).

Chapter 4

Writing with Authority
Ethos and the Seminar Essay
Elizabeth Vogel

When beginning your first graduate seminar paper, you might wonder how you will be able to write about a topic with only the knowledge of a fifteen-week seminar. When you do so, you are thinking about your ethos. Ethos is the ethical stance of a writer/speaker, but it also conveys authority and credibility. It determines whether a reader is willing to read the author's writing or whether an audience is willing to listen to a speaker. Understanding ethos is essential to your academic writing, both as a graduate student and as a future professional in the field.

Creating authority when entering a new discourse community is not always an easy transition. Although graduate students are not entering the academy for the first time, English studies at the graduate level is a new discourse community with its own expectations. How does one speak from a place of authority without actually having a great deal of it within the subject of study? That is, how does one become an insider in a discourse community without actually being one?

Creating ethos occurs in conceptual ways and also via practical steps that communicate authority and establish trust between author and reader. There are a few strategies that help a student make the leap from outsider to insider status. Here is a list of ways an author can communicate with authority:

- Word choice: try not to repeat the same words or expressions. Novice writers tend to repeat language. This is both a stylistic problem and a conceptual black hole. Repeated language is clunky, but it also keeps the

ideas from moving the argument forward. One recommendation is to circle repeated language once a draft is finished in order to become aware of how this repetition affects your argument.
- Know the texts you are discussing. Take notes on the texts you are using.
- Know the quality of the scholarship you are using. Make sure you are using credible sources.
- If you are discussing a particular topic, try to read "works cited" or "references" sections to discover which scholars should be consulted. Read and include them. This process will teach you the essentials of academic discussion. Structure your paper properly so that your argument is clear.
- Avoid words such as "never" or "always." These are claims that you probably cannot make.
- Try to cultivate a belief in what you have to say. Your scholarly expertise and confidence can feel like a developmental leap at this stage in your professional career—but that is to be expected.
- Write well! Just the overall quality of your writing can help you establish your ethos and convince a reader to read your words.

One concrete example of imagining or inventing ethos is the dissertation proposal. When graduate students write a dissertation proposal, they must imagine they are as knowledgeable about the topic at the beginning of the writing process as they will be at the end of it. The dissertation might take one or several years to complete. Because of the research writing process, the person who defends his/her dissertation is an expert on the subject matter. The person writing the proposal must imagine that one knows as much about the material as the person at the end of the process.

As academic writers know, changes occur over time during the research process. Some ideas are discarded and some are expanded. Chapters in the dissertation may be altered during writing and researching as the writer becomes more knowledgeable about the topic. Certain sections or chapters can be eliminated entirely. This is all an expected part of the process.

If the finished dissertation ends up being different from the proposal, and if the writer doesn't know everything about the topic before writing that proposal, how does he/she cultivate sufficient ethos to write the proposal? This is a perfect example of invented or imagined ethos. The writer must write "as if" one is writing from the place of the finished dissertation. The writer must imagine that one has already read, sifted through, and analyzed the material and is the expert on the topic. The writer must catapult one's imagination to the end product.

To accomplish this authentically seems a daunting task. This author needs to be sincere, trustworthy, authoritative, and credible—all without having an all-encompassing grasp of the material. The student must undertake as much research as possible to obtain knowledge of the subject matter and then apply the stylistic indicators of authority discussed above. The student must then imagine and act "as if" one knows all the required knowledge that will be available at the end of the dissertation, even at the outset.

Creating a strong ethos will become integral to your writing voice as you obtain more knowledge of your discipline. After a few years of writing scholarship, you may not have to think about it at all. Until then, you can make rhetorical choices in your writing that will strengthen your authority and impact your readers. Eventually, expressing yourself in a confident, scholarly voice will become second nature to you and inform how you think and write.[1]

NOTE

1. A companion to this piece, in which these issues are explored at greater length, appears at gradseminar.com.

Chapter 5

A Scaffold for Scholarship
Revising the Seminar Writing Assignment
Janet G. Auten

The seminar paper assignment rests on a deceptively plain idea: a writing prompt must function differently from a test question—which simply seeks to find out what students have learned. At the graduate level, students should be testing out their own ideas in their writing. Rather than writing "an answer" to a question, as on an essay exam, students should respond to an effective writing assignment with exploration, even theorizing. They might locate their scholarly selves, find a path in a forest of competing theories, perhaps make a personal connection to course material in the process of writing.

This chapter addresses the need to carefully structure seminar writing assignments to foster the intellectual growth of graduate students as scholars. It uses both published research in writing studies and comments collected over a decade from students in a graduate teaching seminar to picture the context of material and intellectual conditions in which graduate students receive an assignment. This contextualizing calls for a structured approach to the assignment that redefines its impetus as an intellectual project, suggesting a sequence of scholarly activities that both feed into and function as part of the work of scholarship.

By expanding the goals of seminar writing beyond a "term paper" assignment, faculty can help students find their way in academic professionalism. A meaningful sequence of writing tasks, this *scaffold for scholarship* invites rather than demands that students engage in professional activity by:

- fostering effective scholarly habits of research, reflection, and revision,

- helping students understand scholarly genres such as abstracts and bibliographies, and
- furnishing experience in operating within a scholarly community and collaborating with peers.

Such a writing project helps students make the transition from schoolwork to scholarship, demonstrating a process that rests on a new set of three Rs: responding, researching, and reflecting.

GRADUATE STUDENT WRITERS AS NOVICE SCHOLARS

A problem with the standard scenario of assigning a seminar paper lies within its underlying assumption that graduate students come to the course fully ready to write the kind of scholarly paper it envisions. Research on the writing habits and attitudes of graduate students is scant, but it consistently shows that writing a seminar paper presents a challenge to most graduate students for which they are underprepared (Caffarella and Barnett 2000; Lavelle and Bushrow 2007).

Much research on graduate student writing has focused on supporting international students, for many of whom English is not a native language. More recent work has underscored the fact that graduate-level writing challenges all graduate students, an inescapable reality that academic writing *has* no "native speakers." Still, often in graduate programs, "writing is seen as 'a problem' in need of fixing," and graduate students must rapidly (and simultaneously) "(1) become discourse analysts; (2) develop authorial voice and identity; and (3) acquire critical competence" on their own time (Badenhorst et al. 2015, 1).

Many students struggle to meet these new academic challenges while facing high, but often tacit, expectations about their competence in writing for an academic audience. Caffarella and Barnett (2000) and other scholars found a prevailing assumption among faculty that graduate students already had acquired the skills necessary to write like scholars.

Meanwhile, students themselves may feel confident in "writing papers" for college courses, unaware that "the complexity of writing at the graduate level demands that students move beyond the strategies of their undergraduate years" (Lavelle and Bushrow 2007, 818). As a student in the 2015 graduate teaching seminar reflected:

> College did not prepare me to write an academic paper. . . . I wasn't conditioned to ask questions of the text or the larger context. I see now that my encounter with writing an analysis was largely a static one during college, not viewing texts or ideas as a means of changing [my ideas] but as a means of getting a grade.

Confounded by false confidence from years of writing in school, students encounter anxiety and confusion about graduate-level assignments that ask for analysis and reflection on research. The resulting miasma of misunderstanding can derail both faculty effectiveness and student efforts to generate scholarly discourse.

The problem is exacerbated by the fact that while students may have missed training in academic writing, they now find themselves busy adults with jobs, families, and responsibilities that take them away from classroom concerns. They may see the time for prewriting and rewriting, careful editing and revision, as a luxury they cannot afford. Pressure to produce work to meet deadlines as well as expectations of excellence in their chosen field of study puts students' ability to churn out acceptable undergraduate-level "term papers" to the test:

> [because] a significant difference exists between scholarly writing style and term paper writing style . . . [they may] become immersed in jargon, fragmented ideas, unsupported opinions, and a disorganization "fog." . . . Fearful that they will leave an important point out, they spill every thought on the page. (Harris 2006, 136)

The reality becomes clear when instructors face yet another batch of substandard seminar papers—to which they must assign substandard grades.

It is important to understand this context in which students receive and respond to writing assignments in order to be able to create conditions that can help them not only succeed in writing for the seminar but also establish a firm footing in scholarly writing. The lack of training and the time pressures that plague graduate writing can be addressed through wise structuring of assignments, breaking down the monolithic semester writing assignment into manageable pieces, and providing an instructive variety of scholarly tasks.

SCAFFOLDING SCHOLARSHIP

Research shows a compelling need to offer graduate students opportunities to study and practice the scholarly methods and techniques they must learn in order to join the work of the academy. Setting aside the familiar complaint that "it's not our job to teach writing," graduate faculty can offer important mentoring through writing assignments that guide students in both planning for and engaging in reading, research, and writing as *one coherent process*. Instead of explicit writing instruction in the classroom, instructors can offer students support "in a systematic way at the very point where scholarly style and identity is being shaped" (Rose and McClafferty 2001, 27) by means of a sequence of assignments.

This carefully structured set of writing tasks, as outlined below, provides a framework or "scaffold"[1] that aims at building students' confidence along with their learning. Thus it can operate as a form of writing instruction to lead students beyond the boundaries of traditional school-sponsored production toward deep learning and theorizing. Meanwhile, it offers students some practical experience of writing in the scholarly genres they will need as functioning scholars.

Scholarly writing already operates as a system of tiered tasks that build upon each other, from abstract writing, to critiques and literature reviews, to more complex tasks such as grant proposals and reports, researched essays, and journal articles (Harris 2006). As we have seen, "merely reporting or 'summarizing' are insufficient. Graduate writers must often integrate disparate ideas, synthesize perspectives, and extend theory" in their writing, tasks that demand higher-level skills they may lack (Lavelle and Bushrow 2007, 809).

A scaffolded, semester-long writing sequence addresses that gap by guiding students in stages, from observing and recording ideas to analysis and comparison of theories and finally toward thinking and theorizing of their own. It shows students how to pursue a scholarly project rather than focusing solely on a product. The sequence starts with active learning and reflecting on reading in a *response journal*, which acts as a bridge between the student and academic discourses. The next assignment, an *annotated bibliography*, brings in students' own academic interests and calls for critical thinking about texts. It also models an essential scholarly skill: analyzing different perspectives on a topic and making an objective assessment of sources. Lastly, students are asked to draw on their reflective reading and evaluation of sources as they write a *researched essay* to cap the sequence.

Embedded in all of these writing projects is a call for *reflection* as a way to make sense of experience. Its metacognitive blend of self-examination and analysis asks for higher-level thinking, and students may need a precisely worded prompt to write a reflection piece on their work. For example, questions such as "What was the most challenging part of this assignment for you? What did you most enjoy about writing this?" help students assess their own process and also think about their learning. It might include a question such as "How do you see this paper advancing your work in the course?" or "How did this assignment complicate or support your understanding of our course material?" While especially vital for future teachers in a pedagogy seminar, such an assessment question can give any graduate student a practical perspective on coursework and learning. At the end of one of these papers, a student remarked on this new way of looking back on his work, saying that he was surprised to realize that "only through reflection and a sort of interior meditation" did he come to understand the material.

ASSIGNMENTS FOR ADULTS

Starting with a one-page summary in the syllabus,[2] the semester writing sequence keeps pace with the course through clear guidelines and carefully crafted assignment sheets. In creating these assignments, professors must maintain the same sense of audience and purpose they expect of students. Expectations, including evaluation criteria, must be explicit.

As a student in the 2016 seminar concluded bluntly,

> Graduate students still need several deadlines so that each step of the process is given ample time. Assuming that students with a range of curricular and extra-curricular obligations will plan their time without those guides is foolhardy.

The same student added a wry note to himself as a future teacher: "It is valuable to assume nothing about students. I was a well prepared college student coming into graduate school and I still had difficulty finding my research bearings." An assignment sheet must also offer students a clear idea of how the assigned task fits into the course and draws on the previous writing tasks as well as a description of the requirements, content, and format.

From the outset, these assignments are framed using the popular Bakhtinian perspective on scholarship as a collection of various voices engaged in dialogue. A compelling analogy between entering the academy and entering a "conversation" comes from influential rhetoric scholar Kenneth Burke. Burke famously pictured a scholarly community as a group of guests in a "Parlor," an engaging yet profound way of talking about academic writing that appeals strongly to students.[3] Late in the semester, a student commented about the way, working within this potent metaphor of "joining the conversation," she

> felt empowered to be part of the academic discourse, regardless of whether or not this essay sees a larger audience. I felt like it prepared me for being invested in a career as an academic, prepared to argue my case and further the discourse with my peers.

As students share ideas from their writing with colleagues in class discussions, the class becomes a community in which students are able to situate themselves as professionals—a community of practice engaged in professional dialogue—where students quite naturally can begin to speak in class as scholars rather than simply students.

READING RESPONSE AS DIALOGUE WITH THE DISCIPLINE

Initially, students may be wary of this new way of looking at disciplinary discourse. The first step in the sequence, a weekly reading response assignment, aims to draw students into dialogue with course reading—and the ideas, claims, and theories it presents. Writing about course reading, the scholarly discourse of the discipline, offers students a chance to think about and respond to texts in a relatively informal journal style. Guiding questions based on a familiar format for annotating sources both help graduate students find their bearings in weekly writing and give them valuable practice for the annotated bibliography assignment later in the semester.

An initial question encourages writers to connect personal experience and scholarship and notice the ways they complement rather than oppose each other. One or two other questions guide their thinking from making personal connections to ideas toward making intellectual connections with the work of the course. For example:

1. Recall a classroom/teacher you experienced as an undergrad that might exemplify Peter Elbow's concept of inhibiting—or enabling—an audience. What role did that sense of audience have in shaping your attitude as a student facing future writing assignments for/in your college classes?
2. Look at how these authors address their audience: How does each try to persuade you? How/where do you see their position most clearly?
3. I think these three texts work well together. Where do *you* see their ideas intersecting? conflicting? Imagine the conversation that might occur if you "invite" the scholars into Burke's parlor with you to discuss their ideas. What do you think they would say?

These responses can be collected and read weekly but are not assigned an individual grade. Students may choose to revise any of them before collecting and submitting all of them for a grade at midterm.

Students submit a brief (1–2 pages) reflection on their progress with their collection of responses. In these self-assessments, the future teachers in the pedagogy seminar are quick to note the developmental effect of the weekly journal assignments. A 2015 student wrote:

> Certainly having your ideas tested by others in dialectical model is useful, but building those private muscles of analysis and synthesis was an important part of my development as a writer. Since the writing wasn't for public consumption, I was able to express some of my responses to the text in a free flowing way not possible in an analytic essay. The job of locating meaning was my own.

A student in the 2010 class mused, "The assignment seemed to ask me not to climb into a pre-existing conversation, but to write out a conversation that I have been having with myself so far this semester." Such reflections on their experience of coursework can help any future faculty member think about how an assignment operates.

ANNOTATION AS SCHOLARLY SKILL

Another way of drawing students into dialogue with the profession is the next stage in the semester sequence, an annotated bibliography. Students are asked to review recent publications in the field and to become acquainted with the principal professional journals while they pursue an interest in some specific topic of interest to them. Focusing students' attention on *recent* issues of professional journals emphasizes the invitation to professional discourse. One student in the 2016 class noted her need for some additional professional research skills:

> When I did research in undergrad, I'd find two or three seemingly useful sources, start writing them up, and realize only at the end of the project that they weren't exactly what I needed. Then I'd either have to go back and find the research I did need or I'd have to reframe my argument in terms of sources I already had.

To help students find a focus, one can provide some likely categories connected to course content, even quotations from scholars, followed by a broad question. But students' own experience in writing reading responses also offers a rich resource.

The assignment sheet frames the task as an important and useful way for scholars to gather and assess sources and provides step-by-step guidance:

> In any discipline, being part of a scholarly community means that you'll need to know how to keep abreast of current thinking and new ideas as part of your reflective practice as a scholar—and perhaps as a teacher yourself. The annotated bibliography assignment asks you to follow your interest in an issue or topic you encountered in weekly reading topics or in writing your response papers.

- Find/choose *three related articles* from recent (2015–2020) journals in the field.
- Create a bibliography of these sources, giving each source at least a full page-long *annotation* based on the questions below.
- Choose one of these entries to describe to us orally in class.
   [Note: if you haven't already, it's time to get familiar with indexes such as JSTOR, which indexes many *professional journals* (see attached list of journals; not all are on JSTOR)].

Such guidelines aim to give novice scholars valuable assistance in finding and evaluating sources in the discipline using methods academics may take for granted.

While many students in the course may be well-schooled in research skills such as finding and narrowing a topic, others may find themselves inadequately prepared to meet graduate-level expectations of research genres such as annotations. The assignment sheet continues with formal requirements and due dates, but it also includes (once again) some guiding questions to help students who may be unfamiliar with the genre:

- Use your thinking, reading-writing, and discussion in this course as a "lens" through which to discuss the articles, summarizing and contextualizing them for an *audience of your classmates*. Why and how does this article seem important to our study?
- Remember that when writing annotations, you must both compress and clarify ideas into an economical, informative, and polished overview—including your *assessment*.
- Another benefit comes from the chance to become familiar with key journals in our field. Did you find this a common topic in journals? Did it seem to spark controversy?

Reflecting on this assignment, a student pointed out, "It's easy for an annotated bib to feel like a waste of time; emphasizing the *research methods* part of the assignment helps students to understand why we're doing this." Another student remarked that "knowing both the names of some useful journals and also the mechanism through which I could access those journals saved incredible time" and gave him confidence in an unfamiliar genre.

THE FINAL WRITING ASSIGNMENT AS "JOINING THE CONVERSATION"

The culminating assignment asks for an essay that synthesizes students' thinking about a topic in terms of their semester's reading, observations, course material, discussions, and reflections. On the assignment sheet, students are invited once again to consider topics they may have raised in their reading responses as well as the one they pursued in their bibliography.

Depending on the time available, a brief topic proposal might be required as a way to help students focus their ideas.

Another function of the assignment sheet is setting a scholarly context. For example, an opening paragraph might explain that

> This essay asks you to take another step toward becoming part of a scholarly community and its professional conversation. It asks you to both pursue a professional concern and share your discoveries with other scholars (your classmates, for example!).

The assignment then gives guidelines, which it may point out are *similar to those found in scholarly journals*, stipulating format and presentation requirements.

Thus the educational aim of both the seminar paper and its scaffolded preparation should become clear to the student writers as the semester proceeds. Again, they are asked to write reflectively after writing the essay, and by now, many recognize the larger pedagogical purpose of the assignments. "We were expected to work from journals that we have worked with already in class, then contribute to a conversation we have all been actively participating in all semester," a student noted. "It was different than other research assignments I've had because I already felt like an authority, having been steeped in the theory already."

This reflection touched not only on the way the scaffolded assignment gave the student confidence but also the way classwork mirrored the collaborative nature of scholarship:

> Researching from a journal that was used already in class also gave me a sense of familiarity with [scholarly] material. I knew what to expect in terms of length, structure, and overall approach in writing in the genre. I felt a part of the community I was researching about and for; I was motivated to find something useful to contribute to the class.

But simply making observations has little significance to others; students must make their arguments count in the academic community. Therefore, included in the assignment is a class presentation, so students "teach" their findings as they share their efforts with the others.

In their widely cited article, Rose and McClafferty (2001) argue that graduate students need a better sense of this academic *community*. They point out that the common practice of prescribing that graduate student papers should address a "scholarly audience" ignores many students' lack of familiarity with disciplinary norms:

> Students are socialized to believe they're writing for a scholarly community, but that's usually a heterogeneous group and, to boot, a pretty inchoate notion—and a hard audience to write for when one is working overtime to acquire the linguistic and rhetorical conventions of that community. (29)

The seminar writing assignments explicitly aim to foster students' sense of community and collaborative work, providing opportunities for sharing ideas, sources, and drafts during class discussion.

A student in the 2010 seminar provided a useful summary of the way in-class small-group discussions of paper drafts provided "a helpful opportunity to step back from my work and see it from a different perspective." She pointed to a more complex function of peer review as a spur for revision, for adopting "a different writerly perspective":

> There's a subtle shift that happens in my own perspective when I engage with peer feedback. My perspective of my own work becomes broader: I enter into more of a "bird's eye view," examining my earlier choices and deciding on an intellectual level whether they're choices that serve the work as a whole.

While many instructors may include some form of peer review in a class plan, peer review functions here as part of the linked sequence designed for a cumulative impact on students' sense of purpose, self-efficacy, and community (see Celeste's chapter in this volume for further discussion of peer review).

An effective writing assignment functions as both assistance and incentive. As journal editors Susanne Hall and Jonathan Dueck put it, "It scaffolds students' work, offering them somewhere to start, a goal, and some raw materials. At the same time, it throws students forward, asking them to grapple with new ideas, methods, and materials" (4). In short, the scaffolded assignments aim to do the work of mentoring novice scholars.

The final essay emerges from the previous writing tasks: the reading journal, where students engage with scholarship and explore their own ideas in response, and the annotated bibliography, where they focus on a topic of personal interest and pursue a few sources for research. Prompts along the way encourage them to take a reflective stance, to be aware of their own thinking and learning.

This scaffold starts where they are, with personal responses to reading and exploratory writing guided by prompts that both support and challenge their thinking. It encourages inquiry, collaboration, and reflective thinking. And, finally, it leads and points students toward writing a satisfying seminar paper that embodies a semester of experience more than performance, a sense of discovery more than definition. One student noted that this scaffolded process helped her to develop,

> A sense of understanding about my subject. An ability to hone and develop critical thinking skills that extend both into myself and outward into the world. A consciousness of audience and my relationship to that audience through the subject I choose to explore. Making something real out of theory soup.

By including specific opportunities for thinking about reading, evaluating sources, and reflecting on the process, the scaffolded assignment sequence encourages students to examine their scholarly strengths and weaknesses and calls attention to the ways a discipline makes knowledge through writing.

In short, the progressive process of "making something real out of theory soup" presents students with a methodology, showing how scholarship works.

NOTES

1. One definition of *scaffolding* is "the effective instructional design that weaves together a sequence of content, materials, tasks, and supports to optimize learning" (Harris 2006, 137).
2. See the appendix at gradseminar.com.
3. See Khan's chapter in this volume for the relevant quotation.

Part III

READING, WRITING, REVISION, AND PRESENTATION

Chapter 6

Setting Up for Success
Strategies for Managing Research and Writing
Marilyn Gray

Making the Grade provides in-depth guidance on writing seminar papers in humanities postgraduate programs. Before focusing on the seminar paper specifically, it is worth stepping back and placing it in the context of the whole graduate program. When humanities graduate students begin their programs, they dive into courses that fulfill curricular requirements for their degree. They become rapidly immersed in new courses, readings, and ideas, and it can seem easier and more salient to orient oneself to coursework alone, tackling one course at a time, one term at a time.

To be strategic, however, it is important to think ahead to the capstone requirements of the degree, such as comprehensive exams and theses, as well as to career goals beyond the degree. What a graduate student would ideally do is set up an organizational system that could serve both the immediate needs of course assignments and the future needs of larger projects. Although some of the information in this chapter may seem simple, perhaps deceptively so, it will lay the groundwork for effective personal organization and project management that will make progress through the degree requirements more manageable and establish habits that will support one's professional life beyond graduate school.

Many graduate students who undertake postgraduate studies in the humanities pursue academic teaching and research careers, but there are other career paths available to humanities graduate degree holders. The research and writing skills developed through a humanities postgraduate degree are valuable in many professional contexts. The best way to position oneself for a successful career inside or outside academia is to invest time developing one's professional skills. The suggestions in this chapter apply to both graduate school academics and to professional situations that rely on similar skills.

BASIC ORGANIZATION

File naming and folder organization are two of the most basic aspects of organizing materials on a computer. Many readings and research publications will come as electronic files downloaded from course websites, electronic databases, or the internet. Very often these files have long nondescriptive or even nonsensical file names, especially when they come from databases. It's best to rename the file immediately and to incorporate author, year, and title information into the file name, or at least part of the title if it is long.

Folders are usefully organized by courses and projects. Each course and each independent project should have its own folder. Course content may be further organized into sub-folders by week or by unit. Some additional folders for assignments and papers may also be helpful. Research projects should have an internal folder organization that reflects the structure of the project itself, such as individual folders for thesis chapters, and that also makes sense for the research and writing process.

Most computer operating systems allow users to search for words and phrases within a folder and its sub-folders. Careful organization and labeling of course materials will make these materials easily searchable at a later time when they may be needed for an exam or research project. When preparing for exams or thesis projects later in graduate school, you would ideally be able to search through course notes and readings efficiently to find relevant material and develop appropriate bibliographies.

In addition to a careful organization of materials, it is also important to back up materials in at least one but preferably two other places. Losing work due to computer or technical glitches can be frustrating when it's a course assignment and devastating when it's a thesis. Fortunately, there are many ways to back up electronic materials free of charge through cloud-computing or internet-based services. Most people are aware of these options, and you could certainly consult your campus's technology support if you have questions. The real challenge is establishing the habit of backing up files and doing it regularly no matter what. Making this part of one's work routine is great for peace of mind and truly rewarding when a data-loss disaster is averted.

EFFECTIVE READING

One of the greatest challenges of graduate school is managing the large reading load that comes with multiple courses. There are times when reading assignments become difficult if not impossible to complete within the allotted time, especially when taking into consideration optional or suggested readings. What some graduate students don't realize is that all readings do not require the same approach, and it is perfectly acceptable, even necessary, to modulate the time and attention paid to different reading assignments. The strategies described below help students approach readings strategically and improve comprehension.

For course assignments, graduate students should keep in mind the global themes and questions of particular courses when reading and consider how readings connect to these topics. When reading primary sources for a course, such as literary texts, graduate students can also turn to established reference works and criticism in their field to gain an understanding of the context of these texts. If not all reading can be completed by a particular course meeting, reading some background material and key selections from texts can be a practical way to keep up.

For secondary sources, graduate students may really benefit from a multiple-pass reading approach. When approaching a large bibliography of secondary literature either for a course or a research paper, graduate students can read sources quickly the first time through to understand a scholar's basic viewpoint. This is done by focusing on the introduction and conclusion, and by glancing at the whole piece's structure.

Once the basic direction of a piece is understood, reading (or rereading) becomes easier because the reader now has a mental structure for processing the information. Alternatively, the student may understand enough from this first pass to decide that the piece is less relevant and to move on to the next one. Selective reading and skimming are particularly important when reviewing literature for a research paper because reading everything carefully would be very inefficient.

Theoretical and philosophical readings usually require slower reading and attention to detail. Depending on how much of this type of reading is required in a particular course, or across multiple courses in a given term, a graduate student may need to allow extra time for these types of readings. For particularly challenging readings, it may be effective to read about them first, using appropriate reference sources or summaries, to establish a basic context for understanding them, especially when starting a new, unfamiliar area of theory or philosophy.

In summary, it is often not realistic to try to read all assigned readings, or at least to read everything carefully. Graduate students should look at the assigned reading for each class and decide what to read carefully and what to skim, or to skim all readings first and then decide what to review more carefully. These strategies improve comprehension and help with time management. The graduate student will also hopefully learn to strike a balance between the reading demands of the course and what readings are the best time investment based on the graduate student's own research and theoretical interests.

NOTE-TAKING AND ANNOTATING

Graduate students begin programs with varying degrees of focus with respect to their research interests. Some enter with a focus (although it may change), while others are open to a range of topics. Once a graduate student has determined a research focus, course readings and written assignments can be used to engage both the goals of the course and the research interests of the graduate student.

When seminar paper topics are open-ended, the graduate student has the opportunity to pursue specific areas of interest within the course's scope. If the course material fits closely with the graduate student's research interests, seminar papers provide an excellent opportunity to work in this area and develop relationships with faculty who may share these interests. Depending on the flexibility of the instructor, it may also be possible to make interesting connections between the course material and research interests that lie outside the scope of the course.

Taking notes on readings usually serves the course context first—what students need to learn for the course in order to participate in class discussions, and what they need to know for course exams, seminar papers, or other assignments. A common reading strategy is to highlight important passages, which makes them easier to find and review later, or to look up quickly during a class discussion.

In addition to highlighting, however, writing a quick summary of or reflection on a reading right after completing it will have a positive impact on learning and remembering the material. While it may be tempting to wait for an upcoming class and rely on one's memory, memory fades the more time passes and the detailed impressions of readings will not be retrievable in the future without rereading the material. Capturing key information and thoughts while they are still fresh also helps with learning new information and preserving it for potential future use.

At the same time that you take notes for course discussion and assignments, you would ideally also engage with course material in light of your own research agenda. When course materials spark ideas for future research projects or simply prove to be particularly interesting, these reactions and ideas are worth capturing in writing. There are several ways to do this. One way is to include these thoughts in course notes and incorporate labels and keywords in those notes that can be searched for later. Another way is to take separate notes and organize them in a folder related to future research interests or projects. Lastly, many graduate students find it helpful to maintain a research journal where they write out their ideas and questions in an exploratory, informal way.

As future research project ideas, such as thesis topics, become clear to the graduate student, note-taking and annotation of sources during coursework can become more focused on how these sources relate to one's own interests. While note-taking to address course expectations and field knowledge will be necessary until coursework is completed, the practice of engaging with the material in light of one's own research interests and concerns will facilitate the process of developing one's own unique critical stance and voice.

REFERENCE MANAGEMENT

Beyond the basic organizational strategies described thus far, there are a number of tools that researchers can use to manage their references and notes. Commonly referred to as "reference managers," these include well-known programs such as EndNote, Mendeley, and Zotero, among others. Zotero will be used here as an example because it is a free web-based application and only requires a modest subscription fee after the user has reached a fairly large memory storage threshold.

Zotero works with your internet browser to make it possible to download references from a variety of databases and other internet research tools such as Google Scholar. References can also be manually entered or edited when downloaded information is incomplete or incorrect. Zotero allows users to develop large bibliographies and to organize them into folders and subfolders, which are usually organized according to a topical scheme.

Storing notes and files for courses and projects in a searchable computer folder was recommended earlier, but it is also incredibly helpful to curate references and materials in a tool such as Zotero. Each reference has a record, and additional files can be uploaded and attached to these records. For example, the user can upload notes on a source (such as a Microsoft Word document), scanned notes, or the original electronic source file for the source (such as a PDF of an article or book).

When a user imports a reference, Zotero will often place a link to the full-text PDF source in the record for a source if the full text is available online. Zotero will not attach the PDF itself to the record. If users have their own version of the PDF with highlights, notes, and other annotations, then it is a good idea to upload the annotated PDF to the Zotero record for the source to keep everything together.

Beyond basic bibliography management, Zotero can be used to generate specific bibliographies for course papers or projects and to create these bibliographies in the style selected by the user, such as MLA or Chicago. Zotero also has a plug-in for Microsoft Word that connects Word documents with the Zotero reference manager. The plug-in helps the writer format in-text citations, footnotes, and final bibliographies in the selected style. The writer sometimes needs to make a few additional edits when the plug-in does not format everything perfectly, but on the whole, much time can be saved using this plug-in feature.

In addition to organizing references and facilitating citation and bibliographies, Zotero and similar tools allow users to develop their own system of keywords, called "tags" in Zotero. When Zotero downloads a reference, it pulls in the keyword metadata from the database and converts the keywords to tags. These tags can be informative for thinking about which keywords would be worth further researching or tracking. On the other hand, if there are too many tags, it's a good idea to remove the ones that are deemed less relevant.

As an organizational strategy, graduate students should consider developing their own tags (keywords) to track references and areas of interest throughout graduate school. For example, as graduate students progress through coursework, they can incorporate readings and notes for courses into Zotero, at least when course materials relate to longer-term research interests. For readings and sources associated with a course (or course paper), making the course number one of the Zotero tags for the reference will also help with future searches for exams or projects.

Alongside these course-related tags, as graduate students develop their own longer-term research interests, they can incorporate additional tags into Zotero to track their research interests as well. When they apply Zotero tags (keywords) consistently to the body of the material they work with during graduate school, they position themselves to enjoy easier preparation for larger exams and thesis requirements. They also set themselves up for more efficient research and writing processes in their careers beyond graduate school.

Developing effective organizational systems for computer files and references early on serves the dual purpose of (1) making information accessible for future needs and (2) reducing source and information loss overall. Without a good system, it's easy to lose references or repeat earlier research because it was insufficiently documented. Effective organizational strategies are critical to successful research and writing projects.

DEVELOPING A WRITING HABIT

Along these same lines, certain practices help graduate students retain ideas for research and writing and cultivate an engagement with their field. As mentioned earlier, one helpful practice is to keep a research journal where you note down any and all ideas, whether in response to materials covered in courses, new topics encountered in talks or conferences, or reflections on research interests and projects. A research journal allows you to capture ideas, connections, references, and other pieces of information as they come up. The research journal provides an informal space for freewriting and exploring ideas without the constraint of formality.

Beyond the research journal, graduate students should develop writing habits that will improve their craft and cultivate their professional practices as writers. Advice books for writers have common themes—write regularly (daily if possible), allocate and protect writing time, allow oneself to write in an imperfect way at first (resisting the urge to edit too early), and build in mechanisms for support and feedback rather than writing in isolation. Establishing a regular practice of writing during the early years of coursework will place graduate students in a better position when they transition to longer writing projects, such as a thesis.

When graduate students have demanding course loads, it can be challenging to envision what a daily or regular writing practice might look like. Here are a few patterns that graduate students could try as a way to get started until they find a rhythm that works. One pattern is to write for 30–60 minutes per day during the week. Another pattern would be to write 250–500 words per day. If courses are distributed more heavily on certain days, an alternate pattern could be to write three days a week but aim for 90–120 minutes or 500–1,000 words each time.

In the early part of the term before beginning specific course papers, writing sessions could be responses to interesting course readings and contribute to note-taking. As soon as topics for paper assignments are identified, writing would then transition to exploratory writing around paper topics or to the actual drafting of course papers. When multiple papers are due, especially at the end of the term, graduate students will inevitably need to spend much more time writing; having a consistent writing practice, however, will make ramping up to complete paper assignments much easier.

TIME MANAGEMENT

In addition to developing a routine of regular writing, graduate students will manage their work much better through some basic time management and planning. At the beginning of the term, when your course schedule has been finalized, all assignments should be documented in a calendar or other time-management tool. Establishing a weekly pattern for completing routine reading and written assignments for each course would then be the first step in planning the term. This approach reduces the time and mental energy required to decide what to do on a daily basis; if the weekly work plan is realistic, then you just follow the plan.

Next, after looking at the major papers due for different courses, the graduate student would create a realistic schedule for completing the research, reading, and writing for these longer assignments, especially those due at the end of the term. While there is no perfect formula for mapping out the time needed for a longer seminar paper, here are a few guidelines to help you think through a realistic schedule. The following suggestions are predicated on the student having read all or almost all of the sources needed for the paper.

Allocate a day or two for organizing all primary and secondary sources and notes so that all relevant materials are easily accessible during the writing process. Allocate an additional day for developing an outline that is as detailed as possible, including references to primary and secondary sources, to the degree they are known. While outlines often evolve during the writing process as ideas become clearer, having a roadmap at the outset will help. It need not be a formal outline with Roman numerals; it can simply be a list of bullet points that sketch out the tentative argument and evidence.

After these preparatory steps, set aside several days to draft the paper; for example, writing four to five pages of rough draft per day. That should be an attainable goal unless there are other concurrent projects. If you are working on multiple writing projects at the same time, then your daily writing goals may need to be lower. However many days are planned for drafting, you would then schedule a couple of additional days for revision and editing, as well as reference checking and formatting.

When planning the work for multiple seminar papers at the end of a term, the graduate student will need to decide whether to work on papers concurrently or sequentially. Working on papers sequentially for the sake of focus is sometimes easier—but does require starting early and sticking with the schedule. While working on papers, obstacles can occur, so having a backup plan, where one could switch to a second writing project while working through an obstacle on the first project, is also a flexible strategy to maintain timely progress. Whatever the approach, having multiple papers at the end of the term requires careful planning and an early start.

In addition to spending time at the beginning of the academic term to plan and schedule academic work, time management should also include regular review. During most of the term, checking progress on assignments weekly would probably be sufficient to make the minor adjustments needed to stay on track. A good time for a weekly planning review is Friday afternoon, Sunday night, or Monday morning—essentially looking ahead to the upcoming week and finalizing one's schedule. At the end of the term, more frequent adjustments may be needed, but with solid planning, crunch time will not be too difficult to manage—with a little extra coffee.

One final thought about time management relates to knowing oneself—knowing during what time of day you have the most mental focus and how much work can realistically be accomplished before fatigue results in diminishing returns. Some people work better in the morning, others work better later in the day. It's worth observing how your energy and concentration levels change over the course of a typical day. If you know that you work better at a certain time, try to schedule the most cognitively demanding tasks, such as difficult reading and writing tasks, at that time. It's not always possible to align one's schedule this way, but when possible it's an effective strategy for optimizing productivity.

DRAFTING STRATEGIES

Graduate students who undertake advanced degrees in humanities often need to change their approach to writing course papers from what they did as undergraduate students. Undergraduate paper assignments engage students in close readings or primary source analysis but often do not require much secondary research. While some of the analysis in undergraduate papers may involve conversation with the criticism, requirements for contextualizing the paper's argument and analysis are not nearly as rigorous as they are at the graduate level.

In that context, many undergraduate students write their analytical essay assignments right before the deadline and without much revision—which nevertheless is often sufficient to receive a reasonable grade. This last-minute approach, however, will not work for graduate seminar papers, which should situate analyses in the field's scholarly conversations. Graduate students will spend substantially more time on research and writing in order to respond to and integrate the ideas of other scholars.

Writing more complex papers will require a combination of outlining, multiple drafts, and substantial revision. More time invested in outlining may help reduce the amount of revision, but detailed outlines can be difficult to construct at the very beginning of the paper. Sometimes writers must write themselves into their arguments, which means engaging in more exploratory writing before starting a formal draft, as well as working through multiple revisions along the way to a final draft.

While this chapter does not address drafting techniques in detail, a few tips will be noted. First, if the writing process starts without an outline or with only a rough outline, then it's a great idea to construct an outline based on the rough draft later in the process after a draft (or a portion of a draft) has been written. This technique is called "reverse outlining" because it involves outlining from a written text rather than creating an outline before drafting a text.

Another tip is to conceptualize your draft as having several stages: the first (and roughest) one is the "brain dump" stage, then comes the intermediate stage, when you revise globally for paragraph structure and content, and then the final stage, where the draft is line-edited for clarity and correctness. Each of these stages may take several within-stage iterations, depending on the length and complexity of the piece. One can color-code these drafting stages to monitor which parts of the text need more substantive work and which parts only need final editing. Once a section has been sufficiently edited, it can be color-coded to signal that this part can be left alone while other sections of the essay are further revised.

A final suggestion is to save successive drafts (and number or date them) rather than repeatedly overwrite a single Word file. It's entirely possible to change one's mind about the direction or the argument of a paper multiple times. If you have saved successive drafts, then you have the option of returning to earlier versions or of recovering paragraphs or sections that might have been edited out at some point. At any rate, it's helpful to have a full record of the paper's development up to the point it is completely done. Once you have finished the paper, then you can decide whether to keep the earlier drafts or delete them.

PROJECT MANAGEMENT

Thus far, this chapter has addressed several topics—organization, time management, reference management, and drafting tips—that, taken together, could be understood as project management for academic research and writing. While project management in business and other contexts includes management of teams and financial targets, many of the activities an academic undertakes to manage research and writing relate to the skill set of project management. Project management as such, however, is rarely discussed in academic contexts and remains a relatively occluded aspect of academic professional development.

As graduate students progress beyond coursework into more challenging requirements such as the thesis, organizational practices for managing research and writing will become more critical to achieving goals in a timely manner. For example, managing citations for a seminar paper may be feasible through simple file organization and careful note-taking. However, as projects become larger, it becomes more challenging and less efficient not to use a tool such as a reference manager. It is also much easier to develop an organizational system earlier in graduate school than to try to incorporate it later, such as partway through a doctoral thesis.

When setting up good organizational systems for coursework, exams, and theses, graduate students would ideally consider these skills in light of longer-term career goals. In an academic career trajectory, graduate students usually continue research projects after graduation, while beginning teaching positions, where dissertations form the basis of journal articles or book projects. A strong organizational system begun in graduate school makes the transition into an academic professional career much easier. Project management skills also contribute to successful research and writing-intensive careers outside of academia.

PROFESSIONAL DEVELOPMENT

Project management is one example of a professional skill that is under-discussed in humanities graduate programs. Certain aspects of professional development are not cultivated as systematically as they should be in many humanities graduate programs (Modern Language Association 2014). Even the term "professional development" may not be used as much in some academic circles.

Professional development understood holistically encompasses every aspect of skill development needed to become successful in one's future career. While skills such as critical analysis and writing are highly emphasized during humanities graduate courses, some of the underlying skills and soft skills necessary to future careers are not. Even a central skill such as advanced academic writing is not usually taught explicitly to graduate students, but is rather expected to be learned along the way—as if by osmosis.

What all of this means is that humanities graduate students should periodically step back during graduate school and reflect on their own professional development and career goals. Good grades and positive feedback from professors are certain indicators of success, but professional development entails much more—teaching, administration, leadership, public speaking, and some of the aforementioned skills, such as time and project management. Many universities have programs that support these broader dimensions of professional development, but graduate students may need to seek them out if these supports are not found inside academic departments.

SELF-CARE AND BALANCE

While in graduate school, students can become caught up in its unrelenting pace and feel as if there is little time for anything but academic work. Because graduate programs are so demanding, it is critical to adopt effective organizational and time-management strategies such as those described earlier. Graduate students would ideally also try to maintain some balance in sleep, exercise, and healthy eating. Productivity is enhanced when one takes a sustainable approach to working hard in graduate school. Neglecting health and wellness habits may save some time in the short term, but will negatively impact overall performance.

Balanced eating, exercise, and sleep all contribute to better mental health, but graduate school can still be mentally and emotionally draining. Graduate student life often revolves around a small number of graduate students and faculty, and interpersonal dynamics may be challenging. Cultures within departments vary, and some are more supportive and collegial than others. It takes time and observation to understand the relational dynamics within a department and to decide which graduate students and faculty you would like to work with more closely.

It is important to find supportive people with whom you can study and work. Early on, study groups can be an effective way of sharing heavy reading loads and learning course materials. In later stages of graduate school, writing groups with peers are an excellent way of maintaining progress toward writing goals. Giving and receiving feedback on writing also strengthens peer review skills that are important for academic professional development. It is worthwhile spending time cultivating support systems and scholarly community while in graduate school.

In addition to social support, self-care focuses on how you relate to and manage yourself. In this arena, the practice of mindful meditation has helped many individuals cope with difficult situations and emotions. Simple mindfulness techniques have been known to reduce stress and improve focus. Many universities now have mindfulness programs that provide guided meditation on campus, and many more resources are available online. Being present and more observant of one's reactions to situations helps facilitate self-regulation and self-care.

Humanities graduate students are trained to undertake critical analysis and writing, but becoming overly critical can lead to problems such as perfectionism, procrastination, and writer's block. While some critical appraisal of oneself and others is normal in academia and in life, unmitigated self-criticism and unattainably high standards can interfere with professional identity development as you craft your unique position in relation to the scholarly conversation of your field. Mindfulness and self-compassion are potential antidotes to the excessive self-criticism or perfectionism that can emerge in graduate school or other high-pressure environments.

Self-compassion means taking a forgiving stance toward oneself for not knowing everything and not doing everything perfectly. If you have embarked on a humanities graduate degree, appreciate what you have been able to accomplish thus far. Allow yourself to experiment, take a few detours, and even make a few mistakes along the way. Adopt a growth mindset and cultivate resilience amid your circumstances. As you invest time and effort, you will continue to hone your academic and professional skills, but the task of intellectual and personal growth is never over.

Chapter 7

Time Management Is Everything
Useful Tips for Graduate Students
Natalie M. Dorfeld

The transition from high school to college to graduate school to doctoral studies is an exciting, eye-opening experience. New locale. New friends. New experiences. However, the days of the safety nets (parents, teachers, and coaches), with their gentle, nagging reminders to get things done in a timely manner, have been replaced with rigid syllabus deadlines. Failure to comply with a graduate professor's due date can result in anything from a failing essay to a repeated course.

Because it seems dry in nature, the topic of temporal distribution is often met with resistance, but it is highly effective when approached properly. This chapter provides realistic tips on time management in terms of understanding one's internal clock, visually prioritizing one's workload, blocking off sections for work and play, learning new ways to utilize the iPhone, and teaming up with the best cheerleaders possible to ensure success.

KNOW THY SELF

The first and most crucial step in beginning any project is knowing one's body chemistry and/or preferred sleep schedule: Are you a morning, afternoon, or night person? Barnes (2015) says all humans have this internal clock, which is hardwired into our being and has noteworthy implications for us and our peers:

> People referred to as "larks" (or morning people) tend to have peaks and troughs in alertness that are earlier than the average person, and "owls" (or night owls)

are shifted in the opposite direction.... A lark working a late schedule or an owl working an early schedule is a chronotype mismatch that is difficult to deal with. Such employees suffer low alertness and energy, struggling to stay awake even if they really care about the task. Some of my own research indicates that circadian mismatches increase the prevalence of unethical behavior, simply because victims lack the energy to resist temptations. (Barnes 2015, 4)

The same rules apply to the graduate school experience. Know thy self. For students who bounce off the walls first thing in the morning, an earlier schedule might be beneficial in terms of focusing. Many block-schedule courses from 8:00 a.m. to noon to harness that momentum. For students who roll out of bed after lunch, a late afternoon/evening schedule would be more conducive to their learning preferences. Others with assistantships or full-time jobs must learn to acclimate under pressure, for work and life will always take precedence.

Regardless, understanding yourself and what comes with the graduate student schedule—sleep schedules, caffeine consumption, studying, exercising, and socializing—is the first step to making a plan (see Digdon 2010).

VISUALLY PRIORITIZING THE WORK

In today's fast-paced digital world, the notion of tactile paper and writing information down by hand is increasingly slipping away. Almost everything is becoming electronic, which does have its advantages, but there is still much to be said about physically seeing which assignment is due and ranking its importance. For instance, at the beginning of every graduate seminar, the professor hands out a syllabus that explains the following: a description of the course, books and items required, etiquette rules, important contact phone numbers, email addresses, and, most importantly, when assignments are due. Unlike previous classes, where late work was sometimes accepted, failure to turn in material at the graduate level could be detrimental. Therefore, an oversized calendar is highly recommended, preferably a desk model or one with oversized boxes.

This is beneficial for two important reasons. Firstly, our students are digital natives: born after 1990 and raised with technology. Hence, they are highly visual learners. In fact, they have a 20 percent larger visual cortex versus brain measure than similar individuals twenty-five years ago (see Mall 2012). As a result, they:

- retain 90 percent of all visuals they come across,
- tend to disregard black/white text as insignificant,
- scan from the left corner to the right corner—reading the middle at the end,
- are drawn to strong hues such as red, orange, and green, and
- prefer learning from a visual-kinesthetic standpoint (Mall 2012, 1).

Many professors recommend jotting down when assignments are due and posting this information where it can be easily accessed, such as near a desk, computer monitor, or door. Taking it one step further, color-code these classes with brightly colored markers and/or icons to separate classes. This will give students a "heads up" and hopefully encourage them to begin all projects at least one week out.

Secondly, "to do" lists help keep us accountable. Casey (2006) says unstructured time can often be a painful awakening for most individuals. Eating. Studying. Extracurricular activities. Meetings. Life in general. It all adds up and it can be unsettling to see how little amorphous time we allow ourselves on a daily basis. He states:

> The simple, unpleasant truth is that we are probably busier than we ever have been. Notwithstanding the fact that little science backs up this notion, the anecdotal evidence is overwhelming. . . . Lists are always helpful, but when you add how much time each task should take, it helps prioritize how you go about the tasks. When you prioritize tasks, you naturally focus on those that you can do immediately. (Casey 2006, 1–2)

There is much to be said about visual and tactile nature when it comes to scheduling and prioritizing. Whatever works—calendars, colors, images, Post-it notes, even iPhone reminders—tailor it to your academic preferences.

BLOCK IT

Once a rhythm is identified and important dates written down, it becomes a matter of getting the most bang for one's buck. Blocking off chunks of time can seem very unappealing. Most students view it as punishment: sitting down in front of a blank screen from 9:00 a.m. to 5:00 p.m., working almost nonstop. This is a common misconception. The trick is to allot time for both work and relaxation: exercising, even cat naps.

The first step is knowing the top priority. What needs to be done first and foremost? Vozza (2013) discusses the work of real estate mogul Gary Keller, who looks at his goals and asks, When this one thing is tackled, will it make everything else easier or unnecessary? She relates how he then designs the first four hours of his workdays around doing that one thing. For example, when Keller was working on his book, he blocked the first four hours of every day and used the time to do nothing but write. Early in his real estate career, his top priority was to increase sales. He used his four-hour time block to do nothing but make calls and generate leads for buyers and sellers. By doing this, Keller was able to work very efficiently on the task at hand. He reiterated that "time on task over time—that's how you become a master at what matters most."

The second step is to work on event time. By this, Keller means that most people work on the clock, living on someone else's schedule. They pack up and go home at 5:00 p.m. because that's when the workday is finished. Instead, he schedules "event" time. Meetings. Calls. Emails. They can all wait until he has accomplished that day's most important priority:

> My most important work comes first, and it's done when it's done. . . . The key to making this work and still getting home in time to have a full and richly rewarding personal life is to block time as early in the day as possible. (Vozza 2013)

The final step is perhaps the most important one for graduate students: block in planning time and time off. Keller stresses carving out time to reflect on who he is and where he wants to be: "It's the pause before I hit the start button again. . . . I set aside a day each year for annual planning, an hour each month for monthly planning and an hour each week for weekly planning" (Vozza 2013). This also includes time off for fun things, such as long weekends, leisure time, and vacations. For graduate students, this can be sports, clubs, or simply quiet down time.

So, while blocking off chunks of time may seem unattractive at first glance, it's simply a matter of knowing what needs to be done first, hitting that task hard with no distractions, and scheduling in a reward system. It provides clarity and an effective use of one's time.

iPHONE

"Damn kids and their cell phones. No one interacts any longer. They're walking zombies." The younger generation has heard this before, but like it or not, this technology is here to stay. That being said, let's get the negatives out of the way. According to Julie Scharper, author of "Are You Addicted to Your Phone?" 50 percent of teenagers and college-aged students feel they are addicted to their phones (Scharper 2018). The same is surely true of a large portion of graduate students, especially those immediately entering an MA or PhD program. This kind of addiction can have serious consequences: fewer personal interactions with friends, lack of exercise, even failing grades. Digital addiction by the numbers is staggering:

- Students afflicted spend eight plus hours a day in front of screen, and that excludes homework time.
- Gamers spend 2.5 hours playing on their consoles.
- An average of fifty-fifty texts are sent per day.
- Four hours and thirty-eight minutes each day are spent on the smartphone.
- Seven out of ten teenagers own a smartphone (Scharper 2018, 6–7).

The easy solution is to simply put the phone away when studying, right? Just use the good ol' wall calendar for reminders and make detailed lists. Easier said than done, especially since our tech-savvy students have been brought up with these gadgets since birth.

Instead of fighting the tide, certain apps can help keep everyone on track. They range from tracking how much time is spent on social media to blocking distracting websites at certain times to sending daily, weekly, and monthly alerts when important projects are due. And as my students remind me, the price is right: free.

1. *Wunderlist*: to-do lists and tasks. This app does everything from sharing a list to planning a major project. The best thing, according to our freshmen at Florida Institute of Technology (FIT), is the syncing aspect: it instantly syncs between one's phone, tablet, and computer, so it can be accessed from anywhere at any time. According to the Apple App Store, further bells and whistles include:

- Set due dates and reminders to ensure you never forget important deadlines (or birthday gifts) again.

- Use subtasks, notes, files, and comments to add important details to your to-dos.
- Share lists and collaborate on your to-dos with family, friends, and colleagues.
- Swipe down from any app to get a glance of your due to-dos with the Today widget.
- Save web pages and articles for later with the add-to-Wunderlist sharing extension ("Wunderlist" 2018, 1).

Additionally, when group projects are due, it's often difficult getting everyone on the same page and/or even in the same room. This app allows all group members to share information (folders, comments, lists, reminders, due dates, notes, tags, and even print) seamlessly.

2. *Remind*: school communication. While this app does many of the same things in terms of organization, there is one added bonus: it can translate group messages into seventy plus languages. At a school such as the FIT, which has been voted the most diverse school in the United States, this can be a lifesaver.

Students working on group projects can use the Remind app in their language of choice. The six most popular languages are Spanish, French, simplified Chinese, German, Portuguese (Brazilian), and English (UK). "If their smartphone is set to one of these languages, the app's interface will automatically be translated" ("Communicating" 2018, 1). They also have the option of translating messages, which will help with context and learning new vocabulary. It's a win-win for all parties involved.

3. *Asana*: for the visually stimulated population, this app helps groups (and those undertaking solo projects) get organized, stay on track, and meet deadlines through color-coded icons and infographics. According to the company blog:

> Rather than trying to stay organized through the tedious grind of emails and meetings, teams using Asana can move faster and do more—or even take on bigger and more interesting goals. Asana re-imagines the way we work together by putting the fundamental unit of productivity—the task—at the center. Breaking down ambitious goals into small pieces, assigning ownership of those tasks, and tracking them to completion is how things get built, from software to skyscrapers. ("What Is Asana?" 2017)

This is further broken down into three easy steps. The first step is to capture everything that needs to be done. This includes emails, homework, documents, and notebooks. Under the task bar, it plans and structures work in a way that's best for the group by setting deadlines and priorities. This is predominately featured in low (green), medium (yellow), and high (red) bubbles, along with the due date ("Spending Less Time on Guesswork" 2018).

Secondly, after the deadlines are displayed, they are assigned one of the following folders: new requests, in progress, complete, and reference materials. This information can be dragged and placed in a new folder at any time. The layout is clean and crisp, much like a monthly calendar with movable components. "When tasks and the conversations about them are collected together, instead of spreading around emails, documents, whiteboards, and notebooks, they become the shared, trusted, collective memory for your organization" ("What is Asana?" 2017, 1).

Lastly, a horizontal monthly calendar provides a snapshot of what the team must do in order to meet all deadlines. The movable sync bar with the person's face and project information on it provides an accurate view of what each person is working on, how long they have been doing so, and what remains to be done. It even provides cushioning for unforeseen roadblocks, such as incomplete interviews and plans for extra time allotment. There is much to be said for the aesthetically pleasing layout, which is easy for all group members to follow.

In short, the iPhone can be a blessing and a curse. Granted, we may all spend too much time on it, but the trick is making it work for you. The apps discussed—Wunderlist, Remind, and Asana—help streamline projects in order of priority and communication with others, which always enhances time management.

BE ACCOUNTABLE

At the graduate and doctoral level, there is no shortage of "good time" friends who are always up for a party or shenanigans. However, it's also very important that students surround themselves with individuals who will keep them accountable in and out of the classroom, particularly professors and team/classmates.

One of the best ways to do this is to make use of office hours. As previously stated, all professors dispense a syllabus with office hours during which students can meet with them on a one-on-one basis. Although there are many reasons students avoid them—shyness, feeling like a bother, not wanting to look uninformed, not thinking they need the help—in all honesty, professors simply don't remember all their students. In any given semester, they can have over 100 students, with multiple advisees. While they remember the great ones and the not-so-great ones, the in-between ones get fuzzy, so coming in for just fifteen minutes, asking questions, and making yourself known will definitely help your grade in the long run.

According to "Four Ways to Make the Most of Your Professor's Office Hours,"[1] many college students fail to realize that their undergraduate years are more than attending classes and writing essays.

> While these are certainly crucial components, office hours can help you succeed in all of them and maximize your GPA. After all, it's your college professor who's teaching the material and assigning the work. Why not go directly to him or her for assistance?

The same, obviously, holds true for graduate students:

1. Make a good impression: as stated above, just going the extra distance proves you care about your grades, and with hundreds of students every year, it's easy to get lost in the shuffle. Additionally, professors may be able to help you down the road near graduation with lifelong contacts and academic letters of support.
2. Come prepared: professors often use their downtime to grade papers, respond to emails, or work on their own research, so merely coming in to "hang out" is not highly recommended. Instead, bring a list of questions and the draft of an essay with particular issues you would like to see addressed and/or clarified.
3. Write everything down: if something is unclear in class, don't assume that you'll remember it later. While professors are happy to answer questions in class, if something requires further clarification, jot it down. This is beneficial to many international students, who might be somewhat hesitant about asking questions in class about various slang words and time periods in American history, for example.

4. Go often: while "Four Ways" recommends going in every week, that might be a bit much. Students are encouraged to meet with their professor before every major essay is due. For instance, if the paper is due on Friday, see him or her on Monday. That way, the two of you can brainstorm, go over a rough draft, and make any possible revisions between then and Thursday to allow for unforeseen occurrences and/or work simply piling up.

The second line of defense is to join forces with academically minded class or teammates. Again, "good time" friends are easy to find. However, students should also find the smartest individual in the class; if that person is willing to share tips and set up study dates, wonderful. Furthermore, most libraries have study tables where peers can confer about shared assignments. While some feel this is a hassle at first, there is much to be said for the collaborative aspect of like-minded individuals working toward a collective goal of better GPAs.

Therefore, make use of professors' office hours. Roughly 85 percent of college students do not, and this is often reflected in their final grades (Nguyen 2011, 2). Although there are no statistics on the percentage of graduate students who attend office hours, it is surely the case that many carry this bad habit with them into their MA or PhD programs. Likewise, surround yourself with individuals who want to succeed academically. They can often sway the pendulum one way or another.

CONCLUSION

In summary, successful students will know how to manage their time effectively by remembering the following five tips:

1. Know your internal clock; build your schedule around it.
2. Prioritize your workload; use calendars.
3. Block off study and playtime.
4. Make your iPhone work for you, not against you.
5. Surround yourself with those who want you to succeed.

Remember, time management is not about working harder, but about working smarter.

NOTES

1. "Four Ways to Make the Most of Your Professor's Office Hours." *Campus Explorer.* https://www.campusexplorer.com/college-advice-tips/17ED0E8E/4-Ways-to-Make-the-Most-of-Your-Professors-Office-Hours/.

Chapter 8

Peer Review, Revisited
Graduate Writing Groups
Mark Celeste

This chapter outlines some general principles of writing groups as well as some practical tips and tricks for running them. The first section reconsiders the professional and personal utility of writing groups; the second traces the roots of common composition myths and fears that plague graduate writers; and the third offers some specific terms and practices to adopt in your own writing group. The principles and practices outlined here apply to more than just graduate students. From long-tenured professors to all professionals in alternative academic careers, it's never too late to form a writing group.

So please take heed even—especially—if you are not a graduate student: although graduate-only groups, as the name implies, function outside faculty purview, these groups always benefit from faculty support (and, in some cases, from faculty attendance). By providing funding, meeting spaces, and the like, departmental chairs, deans, and other administrators offer young scholars the opportunity to build professional ties and skills that they will carry forward into their future careers, academic, or otherwise.

The guidelines presented here were fine-tuned across several years of experience with several writing groups and workshops in multiple graduate programs. The final section also borrows concepts and heuristics developed for lower-division undergraduate composition courses. Writing groups should not, of course, treat graduate students like first-year writers—but it never hurts to review the fundamentals. After all, many bad writing habits take root during the first semesters of college.

Of course, do take all of this with a grain of salt. As with any guide to writing, the principles presented here are not hard-and-fast rules but rather guidelines that have proven effective across multiple settings and scenarios. Moreover, as with an essay-in-progress, these guidelines undergo constant evolution. Writing groups and workshops, much like the drafts they review, should adapt to their given context.

TO RECONSIDER: PEER PROFESSIONALIZATION

The graduate writing group offers an imperfect but vital form of professionalization: it teaches young scholars how to enter into dialogue about a specific work in progress. Structured graduate-only discussion thus serves as a trial-and-error laboratory in which students hone their skills for peer feedback. Graduate writing groups also challenge their members to listen actively, to hear their peers on their own terms rather than just waiting for their own chance to speak. In official coursework, all students vie for space in the conversation; writing groups, by contrast, shine a spotlight on a single author discussing a single work.

English graduate programs tend to assume that their students already know how to give and receive feedback on writing. This assumption is not entirely unfounded. After all, most English graduate students will teach a 100- or 200-level composition or writing-intensive seminar sometime during their program; marking their way through batch after batch of undergraduate essays, effective graduate instructors learn quickly to prioritize higher-order concerns.

At the same time, many of those graduate students are in the midst of their own coursework and exams, a professionalizing process designed to transform them from students to colleagues. Seminar discussions and written and oral exams test their ability to respond to published writing—often foundational and/or cutting-edge texts penned by seasoned professional writers. (Not all academic writing shines, of course; see below for more about stylish professional prose.)

In sum, then, graduate students frequently engage in dialogue that follows either a top-down model (e.g., graduate students teaching undergraduates) or a bottom-up model (e.g., graduate students responding to tenured professors and published authors). Yes, graduate students informally (and inevitably) discuss their writing and research when they socialize, but the graduate-only writing group productively shapes that experience. This peer-to-peer discourse supplies a "horizontal" counterbalance to the other codified exchanges of graduate school.

As a space outside the pressures and performances of the seminar room, the graduate-only group provides a productive low-stakes environment. More specifically, this environment affords both flexibility and accountability. As to the former, writing groups offer an adaptable forum. Despite the name, a "writing group" can address objectives and materials outside of written works in progress.

For example, in 2019, an English department's nineteenth-century writing group hosted a pedagogical roundtable, sharing strategies for teaching the different poetic forms and genres and histories of the period. Each panelist took a different approach in terms of how "mock" or "meta" their contributions were: some taught a mini-lesson, distributing an example poem and teaching it to the other group members as an imagined audience of undergraduate students; others reflected on their pedagogical principles, tracing where analyses of poetry and analyses of prose converge and depart.

If anything, then, the "writing" element of this group meeting dealt with the *undergraduate* students' writing. Even so, from the discussion, the panelists ultimately carried away several primary examples, heuristic questions, and innovative approaches that have since appeared in their own syllabi. And, as any effective teacher will tell you, syllabi are always in the process of revision. In fact, in the most recent meeting, the group took up two syllabi drafts, discussing not only the subject content (i.e., the readings for each course) but also the structure, policies, and assignments of the course. As this is a document that serves in effect as a contract between teacher and students, it helps to have as many eyes as possible reading and reviewing your work.

Syllabi fall into the category of practical professional documents—a category that highlights the second affordance of writing groups: accountability. Nothing helps you meet a deadline like other people holding you to that deadline. This collegial pressure provides a vital push as the members, say, prepare to enter the job market. This was indeed the case for one three-person writing group in 2018: the group meetings helped them structure their time and scaffold the drafting and revision of sample syllabi, cover letters, diversity and teaching and research statements, writing samples, etc.

At the end of the spring semester, before their first foray onto the market that coming fall, the three-member group sat down and planned out, week by week, target dates to draft certain job documents. They knew their own working habits, they said, and without clear deadlines—and people to hold them to those deadlines—they could have easily spent weeks tinkering with and polishing the same document over and over again.

The post-coursework semesters foreground a certain temporality of composition. Enmeshed in the dissertation process after coursework and exams, advanced graduate students favor slow, careful thinking. Yet, in the words of many a wise graduate alumni, the best dissertation is a finished dissertation.

The writing group, then, helped those three students step on the gas. By the end of the summer they had a full portfolio of documents—something that they fully admitted they would never have produced when working on their own. They would tweak each letter, statement, or sample for each given application, but their structured, accountable work meant that they need not start from scratch when job postings began to appear in September.

Writing groups, in sum, pick up where coursework leaves off. In particular, they help post-coursework and ABD graduate students continue their professional and personal conversations on a near-weekly basis. The semesters of coursework afford sociability: the regular rhythm of class meetings forges solidarity among cohorts, who all face similar academic challenges at the same time. The post-coursework semesters, by contrast, lack that solidarity.

Indeed, ask any students in their third or fourth year of a program: those post-coursework semesters can be lonely. Many graduate students initially struggle with the transition from regular, structured meetings (a rhythm internalized across four years of undergraduate work) to the uneasy freedom of dissertating. Suddenly we're handed the reins, and such independence requires not only self-discipline but also what we might describe as self-care—that is, some way to counter the feeling of isolation.

Writing groups rebuild that sense of teamwork while also respecting the independence of each participant. On a personal level, many students find it nice simply to talk to peers again on a regular basis. Members of graduate-only writing groups often joke (though only half-jokingly) that their meetings function as a form of therapy, a collective gripe session as they face exams, research trips, revisions, and the market.

In all seriousness, it's a powerful affirmation to know that you're not alone in your struggles. On a professional level, whereas coursework makes one feel like a student, writing groups make one feel like a scholar. Perhaps this difference stems in part from experience: of course young scholars will feel more professional the longer they spend in the profession. But there's also something particularly useful in the "horizontal" structure described above. Most interactions in the classroom take shape around the professor. Graduate writing groups, by contrast, offer a more distributed system of social relations.

The point here is not that coursework fails to provide democratic discussions, but rather that writing groups more closely mirror the professional academic interactions that occur outside of home institutions. Consider academic conferences: What are conference sessions but single-serving writing groups? Scholars come together, hear a paper (or read a pre-circulated paper), and then enter into dialogue with the author. All parties benefit.

In the same way, writing groups challenge their participants to describe their work to a wider audience, one not immediately familiar with the texts and conversations. In coursework, all of the critical touchstones come "baked in," so to speak: a small group spends fourteen weeks reading and discussing the same set of texts, and then they take a week or two at the end of the semester to synthesize all of those ideas in a seminar paper. That seminar paper, moreover, has a specific audience of one: the professor.

In the post-coursework semesters, however, graduate students not only lose the guarantee of critical touchstones but also gain a much wider audience (i.e., for all intents and purposes, everyone else in the academy). An effective graduate writing group, then, borrows the mantra from undergraduate composition courses: *always assume the reader is uninformed and skeptical.*

Effective writing groups thus focus on contextualization at two levels. First, does a writer succinctly summarize any key primary or secondary texts? And second, how effectively does a writer delineate one's contributions to the existing conversation? Taken together, then, these foci ask workshopping writers to spell out the state of the field in brief and to highlight the relevant stakes of their present project. Only with that context in hand can a wider audience fully grasp the scope and utility of a given text.

Indeed, writing groups—especially interdisciplinary or cross-period ones—provide a quick litmus test of one's legibility as a professional academic.

At one institution, students from the humanities and social sciences come together to take an interdisciplinary writing workshop as part of a graduate certificate program. At least, the workshop was designed to be interdisciplinary. One semester, though, all of the graduate members—and even the professor—were anthropologists, except for one student from English. The semester, then, challenged that student to build a dialogue across the humanities and social sciences.

In particular, the workshop opened his eyes to expectations and assumptions not only about disciplinary content but also rhetorical method. His readers were variously fascinated and frustrated with his treatment of "nonliterary" sources (a section of his paper featured close readings of the poetics of selected periodical articles), and he weighed the uses and limits of standardized composition structures in social science writing (e.g., the trademark opening anthropological vignette, which struck him as immersive but formulaic).

So while that lone English student's actual writing may or may not have improved across the semester, the way he thought about writing certainly did. As he explains it, he learned to be more responsible when borrowing and repurposing other sources' materials. He also learned to surface the stakes and "takeaway" elements of his work, especially for readers outside of his field and discipline.

Indeed, all writing groups—as explained below—should place particular emphasis on *metacommentary*—that is, "meta" claims about a writer's own claims and rhetorical choices. (Gerald Graff and Cathy Birkenstein memorably describe *metacommentary* as "the chorus in a Greek play," guiding the audience from the margins of the stage; see Graff and Birkenstein 2018, 129.) To help guide extradisciplinary readers, writers should include signpost sentences, spelling out the logic of paragraph- and section-level transitions. Writers should also directly clarify where, how, and why their thinking builds upon and diverges from other critics.

In short, writing groups help students make explicit all of the implied rhythms and assumptions of their projects. Part of the payoff of writing groups, then, is learning how to look at your project from the outside.

This lesson came to the fore in one English PhD program that requires all third-year students to participate in a semester-long writing workshop with their entire cohort. When one of the members circulated a paper on figurations of slavery in a Victorian novel, one of his peers—a nineteenth-century Americanist—questioned the timeliness of his work. The lives and afterlives of chattel slavery, after all, fundamentally shaped the study of nineteenth-century American literature for over a century. On the other side of the Atlantic, studies of British literature had long recognized the impact of the slave trade, especially in texts that might not directly announce its presence.

What, then, his peer reader asked, did his project bring to the table? In the Americanist's reading, the Victorianist writer was merely rehashing old territory. To be sure, his draft did acknowledge recent turns in Victorian studies, but his recap apparently made it sound like British literary criticism was just playing catch-up to its American counterpart. This was not the writer's intention, nor did he have the space (or desire) for a comparative, genealogical analysis of British and American literary studies. What, then, to do?

The professor facilitating the workshop offered some sage advice: choose the debates that you want to have. In other words, effective writing delimits the scope of the debate. If you gesture too broadly and/or vaguely, then the reader will hold you accountable for more than you actually intend. In subsequent revisions, then, the writer clarified the specific gaps in scholarship and how he sought to address them. What he offered, he explained, was not just additional literary-historical content but also a revised methodology for reading presence and absence. Ultimately, then, the solution involved meta-commentary: he needed to make his project legible to a wider professional audience.

TO AVOID: COMMON COMPOSITION MYTHS

In that same third-year writing workshop, some of the peer-review discussions admittedly devolved into what might be called "grab the wheel" moments: instead of offering the given author constructive feedback on what *she/he* could do, the group imagined at length what *they* would do if this was their paper.

To be fair, they recognized this tendency to redirect discussion (and, in some cases, to peacock and steal the limelight), and they attributed "grab the wheel" moments to their differences in our fields of study: their cohort included a nineteenth-century Americanist, a twentieth-century Americanist, a Chicanx scholar, and early Modernist, a Modernist, a Romanticist, and a Victorianist. They told themselves that their feedback had diminishing returns because their peers' papers forced them to move outside of their expertise. They couldn't speak to the critical histories, idiosyncrasies, and current debates in a given field, so they simply imagined a whole new project. At a certain point, they reassured themselves, you need, say, a Victorianist to read a Victorianist analysis.

Yet, consciously or otherwise, they had already proven this line of thinking to be false. When, for example, they reviewed the Victorianist's draft-in-progress, his readers helped him reframe and refocus the project instead of imagining a completely new one. "Grab the wheel" moments, then, reveal not a paper's lack of viability but rather readers' own inexperience in providing feedback.

This recognition informs the next section of this chapter, which diagnoses some of the underlying causes of student writers' tendencies to deflect and redirect. It also provides some heuristics and diagnostic language to help peer reviewers avoid becoming backseat drivers.

To begin, most "grab the wheel" moments derive from the myth of the lone writer. This misconception often takes shape during undergraduate work, when students have limited opportunities for sustained writing communities. Most undergraduate writers live semester by semester, meeting a new group of reviewers every fourteen to fifteen weeks. This rotating cast of readers isn't necessarily a bad thing, but the semester-by-semester timeline prevents writers from dialoguing with a consistent group—namely, one that can see a project develop over time.

As students transition from undergraduate to graduate work, many students thus struggle to resolve the competing chronotopes of the semester and the academy. The academy turns upon slow, careful thinking: professional scholars transform critical discourse not by leaps but by degrees. The semester, by contrast, demands a breakneck pace, cramming in as much as possible in fourteen to fifteen weeks. Full steam ahead, the semester thus encourages writing that works to deadline. Students run perilously close to the zero hour almost out of necessity, with some writers claiming a kind of motivation from the precarity.

Hence the prevalent belief in the lone writer: students sprinting through the semester don't have the time for sustained, truly effective peer review. It's almost always easier (read: quicker) to do things on their own. What results is a vicious cycle: the semester time crunch renders peer review ineffective, so students tend toward isolation during the composition process; in turn, they focus on the submission deadline and never really give in-progress peer review a chance.

Indeed, some undergraduates loathe peer-review days. Perhaps their forays into collaborative composition lacked structure, or perhaps they just think too highly of their own prose. In either case, some students never find the feedback useful, and they rarely take the comments to heart—in part because the undergraduate peer-review process moves so quickly. A mere one or two class periods afford students no profound insights from their readers.

Under such a timeline, comments usually either restate the obvious ("You make clear transitions between paragraphs"), offer empty praise ("I like your thesis"), or gesture vaguely at broad areas for improvement ("Your conclusion is awkward"). Running through such shallows, undergraduate students never really learn what to do with peer feedback. If anything, peer review pushes them away from collaboration.

Shaped by such experiences, many students continue to write in isolation in graduate school. Time management only reinforces this tendency. Especially in two-year MA programs—which move all too quickly, from the students' perspectives—by the time students recognize the potential utility of a regular writing group, they have already graduated. Moreover, adapting to graduate-level studies is a full-time job, and a number of MA students (or PhD students coming directly from undergraduate work) lack the time and, in most cases, the mental bandwidth to run a writing group outside of the demands of coursework.

In addition, graduate students often spend a significant amount of time finding their feet as instructors, often in writing and composition courses. Ironically, though, many of these graduate teachers assign peer-review work in such courses. This decision seems based less on pedagogical utility and more on force of habit: many of their own undergraduate writing-based courses featured peer review—and who are they to break that pattern?

Yet, if those graduate instructors listen closely, they would recognize that another pattern runs through such courses: undergraduates often lack specific diagnostic terms to describe effective and ineffective writing. Far too often they describe their peers' work in vague terms of "good" and "bad." (Every composition course should ban the phrase "you did a good job" during peer-review workshops.)

Undergraduate writers can often nitpick grammatical errors because they have specific mechanical language (e.g., "sentence fragment," "comma splice," and "subject-verb disagreement") for such work. They can also draw upon specific terminology to parse an essay's structure (e.g., "topic sentence," "body paragraph," and "concession paragraph"). But when it comes to style—the subjective choices of form, tone, and rhythm that fundamentally affect the authority, poise, and efficacy of a written work—undergraduate students lack a similarly concrete vocabulary.

This lack further ingrains the myth of the lone writer because it mystifies a key part of the composition process. Without specific diagnostic language to describe it, stylish writing seems more like an idiosyncratic ritual than a reliable (i.e., reproducible) professional practice. As a result, some writers get discouraged.

The myth of the lone writer shares much in common with another myth that plagues the composition process—the myth of genius: the belief that stylish writing derives from inborn talent (rather than teachable skills and heuristics). And when students believe that writing favors genius, they end up styling their prose in isolation, perhaps afraid or ashamed to ask for help. The myth of the lone writer thus also stems from the impostor syndrome that plagues graduate students in particular: many carry the fear that they're "not smart enough" for the rigors of academia. As a result, some graduate writers avoid any show of (supposed) weakness—even something as simple as, for example, circulating a rough draft.

These myths—the lone writer and the writerly genius—can haunt many a graduate writer in complex ways and, in turn, can shut down opportunities for collaboration in workshops. Yet the root cause is simple: not knowing how to give effective feedback—especially specific feedback dealing with style. Without such a vocabulary, readers either veer into grammatical nitpicking or "grab the wheel" and try to remake the project in their own image.

Put differently, readers without diagnostic language struggle to balance micro- and macro-level feedback. One moment they cannot see the forest for the trees; the next moment they try to burn the forest down and replant with their own saplings. Faced with ineffective feedback, writers naturally grow defensive about their prose; some even double down as lone writers, refusing to bring any new progress into the workshop.

TO BORROW: DIAGNOSTIC TERMS AND HEURISTIC PRACTICES

Like any workshop, then, writing groups produce effective content only when the underlying practices are sound. As a group continues to meet, its members should hone the strategies that lead to productive discussion and rethink those that only calcify unproductive writing myths. As in undergraduate writing-intensive courses, the aim is to improve not only the writing but also the writer.

In fact, graduate writing groups should spend time reviewing materials for undergraduate composition courses. As noted above, it's not that graduate and undergraduate writers struggle with the same issues, but rather that undergraduate composition courses foreground the fundamentals and provide structure to the writing process. Specifically, they provide two things crucial for graduate writers: diagnostic language and heuristic practices.

Three handbooks aimed at undergraduate writers—Joseph Harris's *Rewriting*, Graff and Birkenstein's *They Say, I Say*, and Helen Sword's *Writer's Diet*—actually prove quite useful for graduate writing groups. In particular, these books define specific terms and concepts related to structure and style, the areas (as detailed above) where graduate writing groups, both old and new, need the most guidance.

For macro-level thinking, turn to Harris. At a basic level, all writers need to understand the component parts of their essays and how those pieces all fit together. Harris's *Rewriting* lays out three diagnostic terms for doing so: *aims* (a writer's core questions and objectives), *methods* (how a writer connects claims and evidence), and *materials* (a writer's selection of primary and secondary evidence) (Harris 2006, 19).

Writing group meetings should begin with a quick roundtable comment on *aims*, with each reader naming one aspiration or objective of the essay-of-the-day. The actual author should chime in only after all of the readers have spoken: it is always productive to hear others' assessment of what your project is doing (or trying to do). At one recent conference workshop, for example, readers discussed a group of pre-circulated papers. Whereas one author located his work in one field, the other members of the panel located his essay within ongoing discussions in another. Their comments provided a helpful Gestalt shift for the writer: to invoke one of the principles described above, he learned to view his project from the outside.

After discussing an essay's *aims*, writing groups should take an essay's *materials* and *methods* into consideration. For *materials*, consider the writer's constellation of secondary sources: What sense do readers have of the larger critical conversation? Does the author focus on current debates and/or long-standing touchstones? By asking such questions, readers test the essay's *methods*: namely, how effectively the essay articulates the ever-crucial element of tension—what Graff and Birkenstein call "they say / I say." Readers need to know not only what the writer argues but also how and where that writer stands in relation to other authors. The "they say / I say" dialectic clarifies the stakes and contributions of an essay.

In the context of a writing group, then, a focus on *materials* and *methods* raises the all-important "so what?" question. Perhaps more importantly, it raises that question in a polite, professional way. In some contexts, certain comments, consciously or otherwise, come off as too aggressive; the writer, in turn, gets defensive, and the remaining discussion isn't productive. Writing groups depend on professional criticism, and honesty often goes a long way. That said, some graduate students will conflate feedback on a project with an assessment of their worth as a scholar. (Here, the myth of genius and the impostor syndrome again rear their heads.) By diagnosing an essay's *materials* and *methods*, however, readers can point to specific moments and rhetorical choices in the text that could more effectively create tension and signal the stakes.

After assessing the *aims*, *methods*, and *materials*, group discussion should progress from higher-order to lower-order issues. When the focus eventually shifts from the macro-level (the project as a whole) to the micro-level (specific structural and stylistic choices), readers should take the opportunity to assess *metacommentary*. (As described above, *metacommentary* entails "meta" signposts about an essay's own structure and claims.) Does the essay explicitly flag its rhetorical choices? Or does it leave that logic largely implied and unstated?

If the latter, then readers should take the opportunity to ask the writer. More often than not a graduate writer has thought carefully about, say, why one given section precedes the next, or how one example differs from another. Also more often than not, though, that writer doesn't spell it out in her/his essay. The situation may sound familiar: a writer circulates a dense draft—one full of ideas but without clear signposts for the reader. In such cases, readers need to ask structural questions,[1] which prompt writers to directly explain their organizational logic. ("Write that down!" the readers all cry.)

In a sense, *metacommentary* shares common ground with mathematical proofs: even if your final answer makes sense, you still need to show your work.[2] And it's often best—for drafts, at least—to err on the side of over-explanation with *metacommentary*. (Such signposting can always be scaled back in subsequent drafts.) Both the reader and the writer benefit: the former gets a better sense of the project; the latter, through the "meta" act of explaining rhetorical choices, attains a sharper sense of her/his own *materials* and *methods*.

This wisdom holds true for writers of all levels—undergraduate, graduate, and beyond: If you can't explain your own project, then what chance does the reader have? Even if the reader could make safe assumptions about your own implied rhetorical choices, why make the reader work that hard? Luckily, as noted above, an effective writing group will hold you accountable if you overburden them.

As the writing group discussion continues to progress from higher- to lower-order issues, some readers (and writers, for that matter) will have many feelings about sentence-level choices of diction, tone, and syntax—in a word, style. But, as mentioned above, writers often receive little training (at both the undergraduate and graduate levels) in the mechanics of effective style. They lack a concrete diagnostic language. Most graduate students enter peer review with some awareness of grammar and structure, but they tend to think of style only in terms of flashy diction. Indeed, many writers feel the need to elevate their prose when crafting an academic project.

But clear writing, stylish writing, and academic writing are far from mutually exclusive. Style is more than just the icing on the cake: it is the cake itself. And if writers "bake in" style from the start, they fundamentally reshape their treatment of the content at hand. Style is, of course, a personal choice, and many writers—especially at the graduate level and beyond—remain invested in their particular syntax and diction. Put differently, you can tell people that their prose isn't clear only so many times; after a while they're going to take it personally.

When writing groups need to discuss style, then, they should borrow four of the principles from Sword's *Writer's Diet*.[3] Stylish prose, Sword explains,

(1) employs the active voice, (2) favors "concrete," tangible nouns (i.e., physical persons, places, and things that we can reliably picture in our heads) over nominalized abstractions, (3) eschews empty or vague pronouns (e.g., standalone instances of "this," "it," or "that" without clear antecedents), and (4) avoids redundant adjectives and adverbs.[4]

Sword emphasizes that stylish prose is, by and large, clear and concrete prose, and through these four principles, writers can best pursue that goal. Indeed, if you ever have to stop when reading an essay and ponder what a complex sentence means, that sentence is not a stylish sentence, guaranteed. In both graduate workshops and undergraduate composition seminars, Sword's principles help readers and writers pinpoint specific rhetorical choices that add clutter and render claims abstract and/or passive.

By contrast, nothing is less helpful than the standard-issue comment "awkward." This one word gets scribbled in the margins of many undergraduate essays (and in no small share of graduate essays), but writers rarely know how to proceed. The "awkward" simply lets the writer know something is off, but offers nothing specific to fix it. Put differently, the "awkward" comment mystifies the writing process, making style a function of subjective whim rather than (as Sword sees it) an effect of clear, consistent rhetorical choices. Indeed, Sword's four principles diagnose rhetorical issues with surgical precision—a specificity that every writer, inexperienced or otherwise, appreciates.

PEER REVIEW, REVISITED

The more graduate writing groups engage with this shared set of diagnostic terms and heuristic practices, the more they come to understand that effective writing takes place within a community. The lone writer cannot survive in graduate school. For scholarly work, at its core, asks us to locate our work in relation to others: the "I argue" claim only gains traction alongside the "as others have/haven't argued" claim.

Students learn to think by learning to write, and students learn to write by reading others' writing. Writers pick up syntactical strategies by osmosis. Ben Yagoda describes this approach in his *How to Not Write Bad* handbook: reading, he says, offers "the very best and most painless way to absorb the rules of the language." He equates "vocabulary, spelling, punctuation, style, rhythm, tone, and other crucial writing matters" with "table manners" or other norms of social conduct: writers learn better through observation than by rote (Yagoda 2013, 15, 17).

So as graduate students learn to read and read to learn, writing groups ultimately teach them patience. As much as graduate school can mire students in disciplinary and field-based debates, it also prompts them to engage with those beyond their present scholarly circles. And the catalyst for such engagement is listening—that is, hearing the conversation before jumping in. Writing groups also teach graduate students to be patient with their own writing: what writers initially imagine in their heads and what they craft on the page are rarely one and the same—and all writers need time to negotiate that gap. A project always evolves during the act of composition, and writing groups afford the space, structure, and rhythm for such growth.

NOTES

1. For example, "Your examples break with the chronology presented in the primary text, no?" or "Does your comparative analysis follow an AAA BBB pattern or an AB AB AB pattern?"

2. Graff and Birkenstein (2018) provide some helpful templates for introducing metacommentary; see 135–37.

3. The diet metaphor Sword (2016) uses for "fit prose" occasionally strikes one as distasteful (e.g., unstylish sentences as "flabby"), but on the whole, she demystifies the mechanics of style in a wholly accessible manner. Sword has also designed a companion website (writersdiet.com/test): after you upload some writing, the site color-codes unstylish moments according to Sword's main principles. For a deeper dive into the politics of professional academic writing, see Sword 2012.

4. This chapter you are reading, alas, frequently breaks the first three guidelines to conform to the publisher's guidelines. Eschewing the first-person perspective tends to invite passive phrasings, empty pronouns, and nominalizations (i.e., abstract noun phrases that occupy the subject position of a sentence—e.g., "eschewing the first-person perspective" here).

Chapter 9

Presenting Research Ideas in a Seminar Setting

Lucinda Becker

You might expect that you will be asked to produce a seminar essay each time you report on your graduate research, but this is not always the case. You may be asked to share your research in the form of a presentation, rather than simply reading an essay out loud to your peers and academic mentors. This might mean simply talking through your material from a brief set of notes, but it is far more likely to require a formal presentation, to a set time, with presentation slides and a detailed handout.

This need not disconcert you, but you will approach the challenge with greater enthusiasm if you think first about the purpose of such an event. In some ways it is similar in purpose to a seminar essay—it helps you and others to judge your work and ponder your next steps. It also provides an opportunity for your fellow researchers (both peers and established scholars in the field) to suggest areas of development to you, and to share their ideas (and often also any material that might be tangential to their research but that will help you move ahead).

A seminar essay will do all of this for you, of course, but a seminar presentation has several additional advantages. It guarantees that you will have to think on your feet and respond in the moment to a range of questions. (It is far easier to interrupt a seminar research presentation than an essay, so people do, and that is a good thing for you.) By transferring your ideas to slides and having to respond to them and present from them in a set amount of time, you are being forced to interrogate your material far more thoroughly. You will, therefore, start to see your argument as others do, and this will help you hugely in your judgment of the relative merits of different facets of your work.

You will also be gaining crucial experience. A seminar presentation can prepare you for conference presentations, which are likely to become increasingly important in your academic life. You will also be preparing for teaching, which may become the mainstay of your professional life.

WHO GAINS?

Having considered some of the reasons why you might want to rise to the challenge of a graduate research presentation, it is worth considering who benefits from the effort you are about to put into it. Your seminar group will enjoy seeing your work being presented, and the experience will be a way to bond more strongly as a group. Even in a group whose members have very diverse research interests, each member can gain from every presentation. Seeing different research methods in action can save you valuable time, understanding how an argument can be developed logically is useful, and seeing different ways to present research material is of lasting benefit.

Academics know that they will benefit from the experience, too. They will enjoy hearing you talk about your work; it will give them ideas about their own research, and they will be considering how they might work with you in the future. Editors of journals might also benefit. Work that you package for a seminar presentation could be the perfect size for a journal article. Indeed, it might be an avenue of research that you later jettison from your final academic piece, but that you work up independently for publication.

The final, but most obvious, beneficiary is you. Beyond the academic support you will gain, you will also be showcasing your work, and your ability to present it confidently, to your fellow graduate researchers and other scholars. These scholars might include highly esteemed academics in your field, those who have written widely in your area of interest, those who do not share your research passions but who are keen to see how you perform, and also, on a pragmatic note, those who might later invite you to present at a conference or be on an academic interview panel.

If all of this makes the task seem more daunting, you can take comfort in the fact that a seminar research presentation is rarely a negative experience. Your peers will want you to succeed, your supervisor and/or mentor will be there to help you, and scholars are keen to share their interests with you. If you prepare well, you will find it a reassuring and an inspiring experience. That is where this chapter will help, guiding you in how to prepare effectively without taking too much time from your research.

HOW TO BE CONVINCING

A research presentation has enormous advantages over reading an essay in terms of being engaging. Rather than sitting, looking down as you read an essay aloud, you will be standing, head up, facing your group, and referring to well-made and engaging slides. Your voice will have more modulation, you will make better eye contact, and your words will (to a great extent) be those that come to you in the moment. You can also, with experience, flex your material slightly in response to your listeners' reactions, comments, and questions.

However, you must be able to present convincingly, and that means with a level of confidence that makes your audience feel reassured that you are happy to be there and that you are in command of your material. This is not about trying to present the final outcome of anything: it is productive to point out where you would like input and more help, and where you are having difficulties seeing your way through the analysis to your next step, but this must be grounded in a confidence that you have done the work and have the ability to take it further.

You might expect this to be all about how much research you have done already: in fact, it is largely about practicalities. To be confident, and not find yourself confused or flustered on the day, you need answers to questions such as these:

- *How long do I have to present?* This will never be long enough, but you will need to stick to the allotted time. It is the time your academic supporters have decided will give you sufficient space to present your ideas. When you are preparing, you must always rehearse to at least 10% below the time allowed to give you time to run over a little, which tends to happen in any presentation.
- *How full must it be?* Always consider whether it benefits you more to produce breadth or depth. A presentation on a particularly thorny research area

which you need help to get through may be more useful to you than a more superficial overview of the entirety of your research. In either case, you will impress with your contextualization, but beyond that, consider with your supervisor or mentor which approach would help you most.

- *Do I also have to produce an essay?* In some cases, graduate researchers are asked to submit a seminar essay and also to deliver a seminar presentation. This is not a problem, as long as you do not try to shoehorn an essay into a presentation by simply cutting and pasting sections. You will need to plan for both and produce them as separate entities if you are to maximize the benefits to you from each.
- *Will I be using presentation aids?* You may be required to produce a series of presentation slides for the event. Most graduates find it hugely helpful to use such a presentation aid even if it is not required, as it supports their efforts as they present. Make sure that you know what types of aids you can use: demonstrations, film clips, audio files, handouts and example objects can all have their place in a research seminar presentation.
- *Must I produce handouts?* Handouts can help your supporters as they listen to you, and they can be useful for sharing detailed information, especially if you are expecting questions that require detailed factual answers, but they take time. Take a moment to consider whether a handout would be of benefit, and how detailed you would need to make it; it could be distracting if it contains irrelevant material.
- *Might language be a problem?* If you are not presenting in your first language, and you think this might be a slight hindrance, a handout and slides can help you and your audience to feel more confident about the detail you are offering. Similarly, if your audience members are not experts in your particular niche of research, a handout of key terms will help everyone to follow your presentation. Never be half-hearted in your handouts: if you are producing a lasting record of your presentation, it must be perfect.
- *Who will be there?* Knowing how many people might be in the room, and what areas of expertise they cover, will help you to gauge your material appropriately and focus your mind on how the event might be of particular help to your work.
- *Where will the presentation be?* An unfamiliar setting can be surprisingly distracting, so if you are not presenting in your usual seminar room, take time to examine the room in which you will be presenting and, ideally,

arrange to rehearse in it. If you are a distance graduate, make sure that you have an online presentation area prepared: presenting online from your messy study is going to be distracting for your audience.
- *Will the presentation be recorded?* A recorded event gives you a useful source to return to as you think through the questions you were asked and the suggestions that you were offered. If it is not being recorded, consider asking a fellow graduate to take some notes for you, or arrange to make your own audio recording of the event (with the consent of all present).
- *How will questions be handled?* You will need to know in advance whether your listeners will be interjecting with questions throughout your presentation (which can be useful, but is rather stressful as you try to keep to time) or whether there will be a question and answer (Q&A) session once you have finished. If you have the choice, this latter option is safest, but you need to make clear at the outset that you are happy to take questions, but that you would rather audience members made notes and wait to ask questions at the end.

PLANNING TO SUCCEED

An unplanned and under-rehearsed research presentation is not only a missed opportunity, it is a mishap from which it is difficult to recover swiftly. The academics who are there to listen and support you might not expect to see you again for months, or even years, and so will have a long-lasting impression of a graduate researcher who is not invested in the research or who is not quite up to the task (both of these responses are equally disastrous).

A poorly prepared presentation can result in the opportunities that might have flowed your way from the event (an invitation to join a research group, present at a conference, or produce a joint publication); simply not materializing and—just as importantly—you will have missed the chance to gain valuable feedback on your work.

If this sounds doom-laden, that is because the time invested in a graduate seminar presentation is precious and must be well spent to avoid disaster. It also needs to be well spent because, as a graduate researcher, you are unlikely to have oceans of time to spare. You are researching, perhaps also teaching a little, you might be earning money as you go, and you will be glancing regularly toward your future. This means that you are also likely to be dedicating time to research groups and academic events.

So, you do not have enough time, but you need to make sure you offer the best possible presentation, and you want to ensure that you reap every possible benefit from it. The answer is simple: you need a plan. Moreover, if you are producing a research essay and a presentation, you need two plans.

You may be resistant to the idea of planning, perhaps because you have not felt the need to plan before, or perhaps because you are used to jotting down some headings, with bulleted lists of key points beneath each heading, rather than a more formal planning method. If this is your preferred way to approach a writing challenge, you need not deviate from it too much, but introducing a more visual planning method first will help to slow you down a little, which means that you can feel more confident in your final output. It will also, crucially, help you to see what you can remove from your presentation if you realize you have too much material.

Think of it in terms of reducing the size of a tree or shrub. If you prune a little bit here and there (which you will be doing if you try to reduce an overlong piece of writing or presentation script), you will find it hard work and you risk losing sight of, and ruining, the overall shape of the plant. If instead you simply lop of a branch that is protruding too far (like removing one section of a plan), you will find the task easier and you end up with a better-shaped plant (or presentation!).

There are plenty of planning methods you might use, and guides to them galore on the internet and in print, but it is worth spending a few minutes here to consider how different methods might especially suit your seminar presentation. There are often several different names given to essentially the same plan, so a brief description of each is also offered here:

- *Spider chart* (sometimes called a bubble chart): different from a web chart, this plan begins with a circle in the middle of a page, with your title or key area written in it, and then circles radiate out from it around the page with more detailed sub-points, each of which might also expand into a series of smaller circles. The benefit of this plan is that it helps you think about different sides of an argument and a range of research areas. Sometimes it can become unwieldy, in which case you might need to produce subsidiary plans for each section of a presentation or essay (figure 9.1).

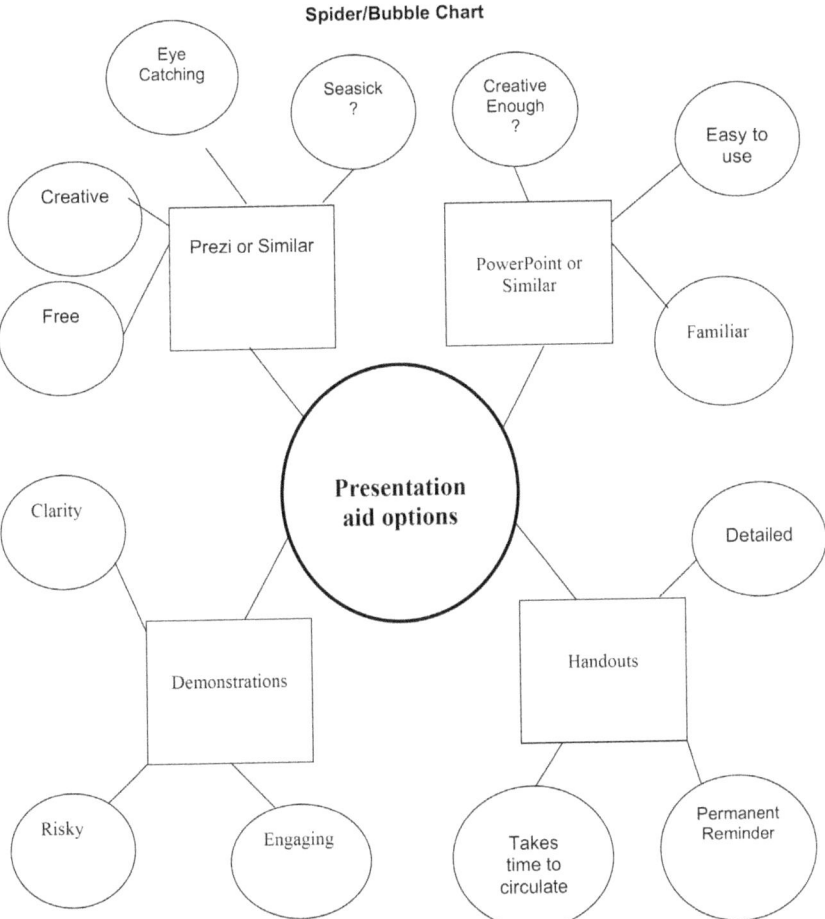

Figure 9.1 Spider Bubble Chart. *Source*: Becker, *Give Great Presentations* (SAGE, 2019).

- *Flowchart*: a series of rectangles flowing along the page with arrows connecting them, sometimes flowing also down from each rectangle to show subsidiary points. This plan is ideal for showing a logical order of information or illustrating a process. It can, however, look so logical that you might become rather rigid in your thinking and find it difficult to change your mind as to the order, even if you have made a mistake.
- *Quadrant chart*: in a square divided into four smaller squares you are able to analyze four different aspects of a situation (such as a SWOT analysis—of strengths, weaknesses, opportunities, and threats). This works especially

well with audiences because it allows you to compress complex information into an easily grasped format. It does not work so well, however, if you have to divide your square into more than four smaller squares (figure 9.2).
- *Fishbone (Ishikawa) chart*: this plan, which looks like a fish skeleton, allows you to note different features that have influenced an outcome, with each feature noted on a bone, and each bone leading up to the head of the fish. It is particularly helpful if you can show your Ishikawa chart on your first presentation slide to provide an overview (which is, perhaps, less easy to do with other planning methods). It only really works, though, if you are looking for cause and effect rather than simply features that are less causally related (figure 9.3).
- *Mind map*: a mind map gives you the chance to produce a pictorial representation of your research. By sketching in images that reflect your thinking in areas of your analysis (including symbols and small pictures within an overall shape or image), it is possible to condense a highly complex situation onto a single sheet of paper. This makes a mind map ideal as a discussion document (e.g., on a handout to remind the audience of your entire presentation), although its connectivity makes it difficult to lop off sections if you find you have too much material. Each mind map, in structure and design, is unique to an individual; you will find your own best mind map layout and so no example is offered here.

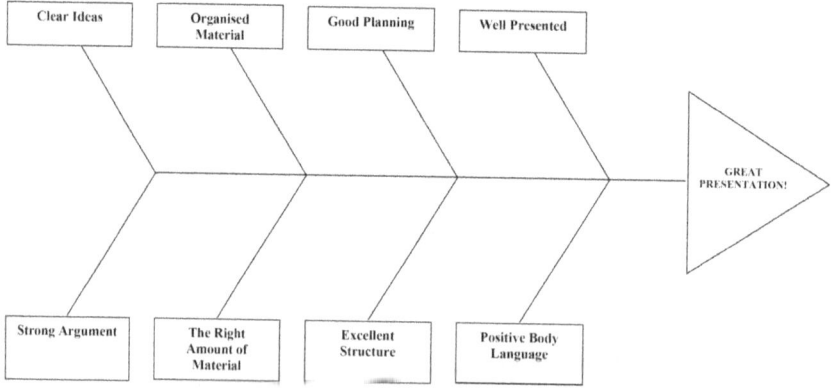

Figure 9.2   Quadrant Chart. *Source*: Becker, *Give Great Presentations* (SAGE, 2019).

Preparing to Present

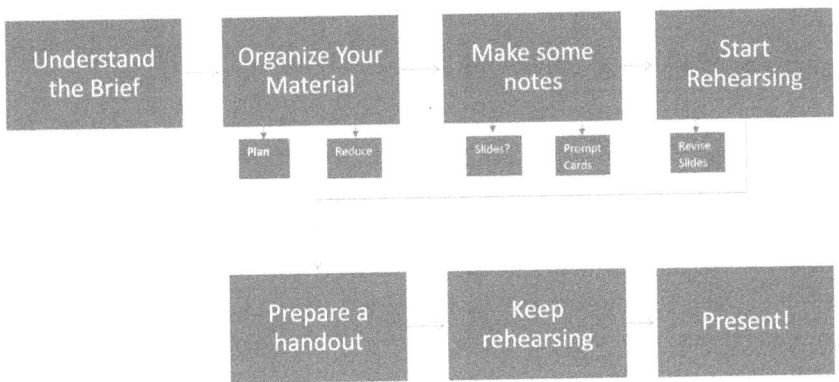

Figure 9.3 Fishbone Chart. *Source*: Becker, *Give Great Presentations* (SAGE, 2019).

There are other planning methods you might want to explore, but those listed here will give you enough choice if you want to get started, especially if you have not tended to plan in detail in the past.

A couple of points to note: for many people, handwriting a plan is the best approach. There are, of course, many planning packages you can use electronically, but, particularly if you think you might need to narrow down your focus, handwriting plans tend to be quicker and more effective. In addition, if you prefer to see things in lists, you might want to use one of these methods but then take one final step before moving on, by transferring your diagrammatic plan to a series of headings, subheadings, and bulleted lists. If this is the way you think best, it is worth the extra few minutes.

Once you have a plan in place, you will be ready to assess whether you have the right amount of material, with a strong flow of points and a logical argument. You will probably want to discuss your plan in detail with your supervisor or mentor, and you may have produced two plans, one for an essay and one for a presentation, so you will want to ensure that the detail of each will help you to reach your goal.

If you have too much material, do not discard what you do not need for the presentation or the essay. Instead, keep it to one side for now. You may find it useful for inclusion in a handout (although this runs the risk of leading you too far from the point by introducing too much new material, so be cautious).

You will almost certainly want to reexamine your plan regularly in the future. These snippets of research, some of which can be delightfully random and seem to serve no purpose except to interest you, are often the embryonic version of a conference paper or a journal article, so they have huge potential, and thinking them through at this stage, even if they are put aside for now, will have been a good use of your time.

HELPING YOURSELF AS YOU PRESENT

Once you are happy with the material, you are in a strong position to start to produce your presentation aids. You then have two more areas to consider: prompting and practising. Using a prompt method when you are giving a graduate research presentation can be a delicate decision.

If you were giving a professional presentation, you might use the notes function in presentation software to guide you, or you might even use an autocue. If you were giving a lecture to students, it would not look odd to have notes on a lectern. At a conference, prompt cards would not be out of place.

Yet this event is not quite any of those things. You might be in a small group, you will want to seem approachable and only semiformal in your stance, and you might be required to sit as you present (avoid this if you can: it is difficult to sustain presenting energy if you are seated). Despite this, you are working through detailed material, under some pressure, and so you are likely to want to make some prompts for yourself.

The need for prompts also reflects the importance of this event. This might be the first time you have presented your research to your peers, or it might be your only chance to draw on the expertise of certain scholars in your field, or it could be your chance to impress a potential mentor or supervisor for future research.

For all of these reasons you are going to be very keen to achieve your goals, and prompts will ensure that you do not get blown off course, that you include all the relevant material, and that you can respond to your listeners as you progress through your presentation.

The challenge you face is that, if you use a prompt that does not work for you, you might run into problems. Even if you have your usual way of prompting yourself in presentations, it is worth taking a few minutes here to consider your options. For some researchers, relying on rehearsals can work well for events such as small briefing presentations to set up panel discussions at conferences or short introductions to seminars. For the purposes of the event you are facing, it has the advantages of looking in control, relatively relaxed, and keen to engage casually with your audience.

However, over-rehearsing might leave you with a threefold problem. It is easy to become monotone in your speech patterns because you are almost at the point where you are simply reciting your presentation from memory. If you have also submitted a research essay, you might be tempted to try to recall it, word for word, and that will probably leave you running overtime. Finally, if you lose focus for even a second, you will forget where you are in your material and struggle to reengage.

Presentation packages such as Presentation software packages allow you to write notes beside or beneath each slide, so that you can see on your small screen what you want to say, while your onlookers see only the slides. This can be an elegant way to prompt yourself, largely because nobody will know that you even have prompt notes.

The disadvantages to this approach include the fact that you are restricted to those packages that have this function. If you favor free online packages (such as Prezi®) you may well have to pay for this feature. If your eyesight is not that good, or you have made the mistake of producing notes that are too detailed or in too small a font, you could be found squinting at your screen as you try to present. Printing your notes, placing them flat down on the desk or table, and glancing at them from time to time can help and also avoid a potential screen barrier between you and your audience.

It can be tempting to produce very full notes, which might help you feel more confident as you approach the event, but this is rarely a good idea. It would be very difficult for you to avoid being too tied to your notes, such that your presentation might become little more than an essay read aloud.

It also brings with it an even greater danger. If you are nervous you might, without even noticing you are doing it, bring this prompt script up toward your face as you present. A piece of paper is surprisingly large when you hold it in this way, and if you are nervous, it is also likely to be shaking: this is not the image you want to present, of course, and your audience will be reluctant to ask questions or query your material if they feel that presenting your research has been an ordeal for you.

A set of postcard-sized cards, with a few keywords or notes on each, can be held in your hands with your audience barely noticing. You can add more than just prompt words: you might write "smile" on some of the cards, or shade in the card that will come halfway through your presentation so that you can check on your timing.

There are only two dangers to prompt cards: you might make them too detailed because you are anxious (your absolute maximum should be thirty words per card) and, in your relief at completing each section of you presentation, you might throw each completed card onto the table in front of you, which looks a little odd. Despite these minor risks, however, this form of prompt has the significant benefit of becoming a permanent, efficient record of your presentation. If you are ever asked to give a conference paper or a lecture, a glance back through the prompt cards from your research presentations would be a great place to start.

If your handout shows structure as well as detail, it could work well as a prompt. That is, if you begin your handout with an overview of the areas you are covering, and you divide it into sections with headings, and perhaps sub-headings, for each of these areas, you are producing a valuable aid for your listeners and also a prompt sheet for yourself.

This only works well if your material lends itself to such a highly structured approach, and if you are sure that you will not want to deviate from the material and order on your handout. You might also consider whether you need to give your handout to the group at the outset. It can be irritating to watch a research presenter who is clearly referring to a handout that audience members have not yet seen.

If you are comfortable with your material, and you have a clear line of sight through your analysis and argument, simply talking through your slides might well work for you. This will look natural and unforced; you will only have one visual to consider, and you will inspire confidence in your listeners.

The only potential pitfall (apart from being under-rehearsed) is that you might make your slides far too detailed, for your benefit rather than to aid your audience. You must stick to the fundamental principles for effective slides: no text smaller than a twenty-point font, no extracts in small print that nobody can read, no images so detailed that they are pointless, no text that is only for your benefit, and minimal punctuation.

If you can avoid these pitfalls, a solid set of presentation slides with which you feel comfortable, coupled with a good rehearsal schedule, should be the first prompt method you try. If it is not quite sufficient (perhaps because you are very nervous or the material is relatively new to your research), you could explore complementing this approach with one of the other methods considered above.

POLISHING YOUR PRESENTATION

There are two key ways in which you can make a greater impact with your research presentation in the days leading up to the event: rehearsing and learning to control your nerves. Even though this is a semi-casual setting, which feels social in many ways, you need to help yourself to shine by rehearsing. Too few rehearsals can lead to a researcher blanking, having completely lost the thread or—even worse—looking mildly surprised as every new slide or handout page appears. On the other hand, too many rehearsals might lead you to seem bored or jaded with the material—which you will be if you have worked through it too many times.

Rehearsals also help to control your nervousness. You are bound to feel a little anxious before giving a seminar presentation, and this is a good thing. It keeps your adrenalin levels high enough to allow you to think quickly and respond to your audience effectively. Your listeners will notice that you are taking this seriously, and so they will be pleased to be part of such an event. You might employ relaxation techniques to help control your nerves, but your main weapon against being overly nervous will be to rehearse well enough to feel nervous, but confident enough not to be overwhelmed by your nerves.

For a conference presentation, or a lecture, you would have a different rehearsal regime; for a seminar research presentation at a graduate level, you would do well to aim for four rehearsals. Each rehearsal will be serving a different function, so you will be able to make use of every scrap of time you devote to this part of the process:

- *Rehearsal one*: this might be a few days or a few weeks before the presentation, depending on your schedule and how nervous you are. This rehearsal is about time: practice your presentation to make sure that you have the perfect amount of material for the time allowed (always aiming to run a little under time). If you suspect that you might not have the right amount of material, you are likely to want to go through this practice run as early as you can, so that you have time to rework your presentation.

- *Rehearsal two*: you will still be checking on the timing in this rehearsal, but your primary focus is on your aids and prompts. If you are using slides, do they work as well as they possibly can? If you have a handout, does it support the audience adequately, even if you have altered the material slightly? If you are demonstrating, does it fit seamlessly into your presentation?
- *Rehearsal three*: by now you have the mechanics in place: you are on the right time, your presentation aids work well for you and you feel confident in your material. (If any of this is not the case, then you still have time to rework aspects of your presentation and add an extra rehearsal.) The focus in this practice run is on you rather than your material. For this reason, it might make sense to ask a few friends or fellow researchers to watch you present, and it could help you if you can rehearse in the room in which you will be giving the presentation.
- In this rehearsal, you will be asking yourself, and your supporters if they are there, how well you are engaging with the audience. Do you tend to smile? You need to, so if your smile leaves you when you are nervous, make a prompt somewhere to do this, or keep reminding yourself on the day as you wait to present. Do you make good eye contact? In a small group this is rarely a problem, but if it is likely to be an issue for you, make eye contact with a couple of listeners at the beginning of the presentation, and this will encourage you to widen your field of eye contact as you progress.

  Beyond this, check how well you stand (not slouching, not leaning on a table, not hands in pockets, not leaning forward into the group, and not facing your slides and forgetting to turn back). Check also how well your voice projects. This is highly unlikely to cause any problems in a small group, but if you tend to mumble and swallow your words such that you might not be heard, make sure that you are standing for your presentation and, if possible, do not use any prompt but the screen.
- *Rehearsal four*: this is your last-minute rehearsal and must be undertaken as near to the event as possible. An hour or two before would be ideal. If you started to rehearse early, there may be some time between rehearsals three and four, but this need not cause you any problems. You are not aiming to

change anything (except any glaring mistakes on your slides); you are simply reimmersing yourself in your research material so that you are ready to make the most of the event.

During each of these rehearsals, remember that this is not a one-way event. If you give a lecture you might simply deliver your material and leave the room. At a conference, your paper will spark some questions and discussion, but these might help others more than you. For this event, the benefit is primarily yours. Your aim is to produce a presentation that elicits questions to help you move forward, and that encourages discussion that deepens your understanding. Keeping this in mind as you prepare will help maximize this benefit.

QUESTIONS AND ANSWERS (Q&A)

Your supervisor and/or mentors will have put some thought into how to run this aspect of the event. If this is your first seminar research presentation, you might expect to be listened to silently, with questions at the end. If you are more experienced, you might find that there are more interjected questions as you present. Neither is a problem, but you need to know in advance what to expect.

If there are to be questions and comments throughout, you can only make the most of the event if you take control. At the outset, let your listeners know that you will be pausing regularly to allow for comments and questions. If a member of the group is firmly making eye contact with you, clearly desperate to interject, just smile and keep going until your reach your planned stopping point. Rehearsing with these breaks in place is vital, so you can feel the rhythm of your presentation when it is broken up in this way.

If the questions are to come at the end of the presentation, make this clear to the listeners as you begin and try, if you possibly can, to stick to this structure. If you are interrupted, you can politely ask, with a smile, if the group member would mind waiting until the end. It feels awkward, but it is usually better than losing your way while everyone else decides to add minor thoughts or questions at that point of interruption.

If you have a questioner who keeps trying to interrupt, or who asks you questions that seem unfair or unreasonable, look at your supervisor or another familiar academic for support. You should find that they are happy to interrupt and deal with the question. Alternatively, you can reassure the questioner that the query is an intriguing one, but not on an area you have studied in detail.

Whenever the questions come, you will be ready for them. You have prepared thoroughly and will feel in command of your situation. However, never lose sight of the fact that this is a research seminar: its purpose is to explore, enjoy, and evaluate. You are not expected to provide the last word in your area (no researchers do that, nor would they want to); you are being asked to show the results of your hard work so far and to share your evaluation of your research material. It is then up to your listeners to offer suggestions, advice, material, and support.

With this in mind, you need to be bold about asking seminar members to pause while you make notes (having also asked a supporter to make backup notes in case you miss anything) and you can feel comfortable asking questioners to elaborate on their thoughts. That is the beauty of a graduate seminar research presentation: you come away with a wealth of wisdom and a store of material and ideas to sustain you in the weeks, months, and years ahead.

Part IV

NEW DIRECTIONS AND EXPANDING POSSIBILITIES

Chapter 10

Digital Methods and Visual Essays in the Classroom

Lisann Anders

Study programs, research, and academic writing have become increasingly interdisciplinary but also multimedial. Literary studies in particular have experienced the inclusion of visual arts, popular culture, music, and film in recent years. This, of course, is also due to the digitalization of society: we can hardly imagine our lives without computers and smartphones anymore, let alone social networks such as Facebook, WhatsApp, Instagram, and Twitter. In order to be able to adapt to these developments, which have seen a continuous increase in the virtualization of our lives since the turn of the millennium, the ways we encounter and treat information, images, and media need to be rethought.

Creative digital approaches must be tailored into teaching at all educational levels as well as into essay writing, especially in academia, as literacy is no longer limited to the written word but also includes an understanding of visual language in the digital realm. Literary studies will serve as an example in the following examination of how to approach intermediality in the classroom and how to craft creative work through digital methods.

Making use of methods from creative writing, digital narratives can be created on the basis of a literary text. Here, images are chosen to illustrate as well as interpret the text. The digital narrative can be used as an adaptation of a work, created by the students themselves. It helps them to play with the content and get ideas for potential papers. In a next step, the application of the skills acquired in the classroom serves to create a critical analysis of literary material and audiovisual adaptations thereof by going beyond traditional essay writing in the form of the visual essay.

Visual essays can be defined in manifold ways: they can be a sequence of images or entire short films that develop an academic argument. Of course, traditional research and theory will not be neglected here but will be included to establish and complement the visual argument. In order to understand the effect of visual essay writing, the latter must be contextualized by means of advertisement theories such as the "Cognitive Response Model" and the "Matching Activation Hypothesis" to show that the creation of visual essays is structured similarly to advertisement campaigns (cf. Tellis 2004; Fennis and Stroebe 2010).

By means of these theories, we can explore the effects and importance of visual essays. However, despite the many advantages of digital storytelling and essay writing, their challenges, problems, and potential solution approaches are also highlighted in the course of this chapter.

VISUAL CLASSROOMS

András Benedek highlights that "the natural way of communication between human beings relies on the application of images, icons or comics where film clips represent an interesting manifestation of unique, relatively short narrations" (2016, 162). Indeed, digital storytelling is nothing new anymore since YouTube, Snapchat, and Instagram. People post glimpses of their lives in visual form and create stories. Social media such as Instagram even include a feature called "stories," where a sequence of images or short video clips can be posted. The creation of digital content for the sake of storytelling is thus no longer only limited to film schools but pervades our everyday lives.

However, in order to produce a visual narrative, the mechanisms behind the combination of images must be understood. Below, I use advertisement theories to explain the importance of image sequences before elaborating on how these can be used to understand literary texts.

THEORETICAL BASIS

Digital narratives are stories told intermedially, which means that different media, such as written text or images, are combined in order to create a narrative. Images are of special interest in this regard due to their ambiguity in associations and their dependence on context. Social studies have long recognized and examined the effect of images and used it in order to explain and predict, for example, consumer responses to visual stimuli.

The Cognitive Response Model (CRM) by Anthony G. Greenwald (1968) highlights that an image always provokes certain associations, which might stem from a specific background, or from the sequence in which different images or text and images are present, or from the context in which they are presented (cf. Greenwald 1968; Fennis and Stroebe 2010). The order of images and text, therefore, has certain effects on the viewer.

While the CRM theory is used to explain consumer behavior in relation to the exposure to advertisement, it can also be applied to the learning effects of visual material. Different associations with images will trigger different thoughts on the content of the images and image sequences, allowing for individual perception and yet a critical thought process as well.

While this holds true for all text, not only visuals, the Matching Activation Hypothesis (MAH) looks at the relation of image and text and how these two media forms influence each other with regard to the viewer's or reader's perception.

> The matching activation hypothesis predicts that the greater activation of the right (left) hemisphere during the processing of attended pictorial (verbal) information could enhance the processing of additional material represented within the left (right) hemisphere, provided the material in the opposing hemisphere can be processed by that hemisphere. (Janiszewski 1990, 54)

In other words, the combination of text and image can help process the content of both media forms better, which in turn helps one gain a deeper understanding of the material.

Because the response to image and text is affected by putting them in relation to each other, the sequence and the context of the images then trigger how the message is received. We have different associations with images in different textual contexts and, depending on the order of images, we arrive at a different conclusion, which is called *message structure*: "Message structure refers to *how* a product is communicated and thus to the order of presentation" (Fennis and Stroebe 2010, 18).

The MAH and message structure can be best explained by means of an example from advertising. Advertisements are usually carefully placed in, for instance, newspapers and magazines. They sometimes relate to the content of the written text in order to draw immediate connections between the two, and if they are not related, they still evoke associations.

This can also mean, however, that an advertisement can be misplaced by accident; that is, that the effect of either text or advertisement is not the positive response expected because neither the image nor the text match or they match in a way the advertisers did not intend (figures 10.1, 10.2, and 10.3).

The newspaper article from *The Brampton Guardian* uses an image that is related to the text as the site of destruction caused by two vandals. However, since the image shows two figures and the title is about a "crime duo caught on video," these two figures are associated with the two criminals. The reader thus expects to see the vandals in the image, since they were "caught on video."

Figure 10.2 of the *Belfast Telegraph* shows a sinking ship in reporting on the search for survivors, but the newspaper places an advertisement above it that appears to be an ironic comment on the image. The promoted "dream holiday" of the advertisement takes an ironic turn when we glance at the image below it, since the capsized ship is a cruiser and its passengers' dream holiday turned into a nightmare.

Figure 10.3 of *The Daily Telegraph* also relates two images that were not intended to be paired. The image shows the Queen, Camilla Parker-Bowles (wife of the Prince of Wales), and the Duchess of Cambridge (wife of William, the Queen's grandson). The article, on the other hand, is about the possible dangers of children being exposed to the idea of witches. However, the unfortunate placement of the picture above the text associates witches to the

Figure 10.1 "Violent Crime Duo." *Source: The Brampton Guardian* (January 13, 2012).

Figure 10.2 "**Dream Holiday.**" *Source*: *Belfast Telegraph* (January 16, 2012).

three royals. These examples show how images and text are dependent on each other since they trigger associations in the viewer.

In order to apply these ideas to literary studies, the genre of the crime novel or crime TV show will serve as an example in terms of plot structure, which offers two possible approaches. On the one hand, we can start with the murder, knowing who the murderer is and watch how the police will unravel the case; on the other hand, we can follow the classic whodunit structure, in which we start at the crime scene and trace the clues to the murderer. If these were translated into images, we would either have the sequence of a photo of a crime scene, followed by, for instance, the murder weapon, or vice versa, as in example two.

The narrative structure is thus inverted by the image sequence. While this is especially important in digital storytelling, it is also useful to be aware of context and of the sequence of images and text, especially in the creative production of critical analyses of image and text. Below I introduce some methods in which theoretical knowledge of the CRM and the MAH can be useful in better understanding a literary work in which image-text relations are created.

138 Lisann Anders

Figure 10.3 "Witchcraft." *Source: The Daily Telegraph* (March 2, 2012).

VISUAL TEACHING AND LEARNING

Working with images implies more than merely using images to illustrate a text. Images can be read as texts, too. Alexandra Howson confirms this use of images by inferring that "images do not merely illustrate the topic under investigation, but are the media through which analysis proceeds" (2008, 44). She further explains that "Academic feminism has challenged the centrality of text in knowledge production and has sought to create pedagogical strategies that explore innovative methods of teaching and learning through nonconventional methods such as poster presentations" (57).

Images are thus not only an entertaining way of exploring literary texts and other forms of media, but also a means of analysis (cf. 47). To use images within the scope of the classroom, be it in literature, popular culture, or film, Howson's introduction of poster presentations can be followed as a first step. However, in contrast to her elaborate poster assignment as an alternative to a written analysis, I would suggest beginning with an advertisement poster for the work studied in the course. This can be in the form of film posters or book covers, depending on the type of work and medium being examined.

For example, if Shakespeare's *Macbeth* is discussed in class, the students are given the task of creating a performance poster, summing up the essence of the plot in a single image while also catching the attention of a potential audience. Here, the media theories outlined above present a solid basis for understanding how to present the poster and what the intended effect should be—and what mistakes to avoid.

Posters can be in color or black and white, can feature a quotation from the play and/or present a key moment. On a *Macbeth* poster, we could thus find a half-transparent dagger or a bloody crown with the Weïrd Sisters' spell, "Double, double toil and trouble" (*Macbeth* 4.1.20). Such posters help to translate the core of a text into a visual medium. Furthermore, they already hint at the manifold ways of interpreting this core, as every poster will display a different aspect of the play.

Another form of working with visuals and texts is to create advertisement slogans for the play. This exercise is very similar to the poster but emphasizes the text again, in which the image only supports the written word, in contrast to the poster, in which the text supported the image. These advertisement slogans can be visualized in the form of bumper stickers, for instance. The slogan again helps students to think about the play and characters in a creative way and adds a subjective perspective, one that will be important once again for the essay—be it traditional or visual.

Of course, these exercises can be done at various levels of studies, that is, the secondary and tertiary education levels. While this seems almost trivial for postgraduates, it remains a playful form of engaging with the text and discovering aspects that might have been overlooked otherwise. Moreover, the visual component helps to grasp the text at a representational level.

This way of representation can also be taken a step further by transposing the text into digital images. This can be done, for example, by means of emojis. The plot of a play needs to be described only by the language of visual icons, without adding any text. This exercise encourages students to walk through the different scenes of a play and helps the teacher to see potential difficulties students face at the plot level. To visualize this type of translation, an icon summary for *Macbeth* could look something like the one shown in figure 10.4.

This digital approach allows one to see difficulties but also opportunities in visual representations of text. For instance, it shows that some plot lines are not easy to visualize, such as Lady Macbeth's madness or Macbeth's confidence that he cannot be defeated. A character's development is thus harder to represent than simple actions and events.

If a close reading of scenes is required, digital means can also help to better grasp the characters and events of scenes. Here, social media can be of some use, as this is a prevalent means of communication in our digital age: "visual learning carries the possibility of such parables that will be able to improve the efficiency of human learning, currently characterised by a constant lack of time and information pressure" (Benedek 2016, 161).

Therefore, by using social media platforms that students engage with on a daily basis, a work's scenes, characters, and language can be rendered more approachable—especially if the language is as demanding as early modern English. The Cambridge Blog has reimagined Shakespeare's *Romeo and Juliet* and has translated various scenes into social media, as illustrated by the examples in figures 10.5 and 10.6.

The Twitter example (figure 10.5) shows that by choosing nicknames for the characters, the latter are already characterized to a certain extent, whereas the example of the text exchange between Romeo and Juliet (figure 10.6) highlights the play's problems of communication. These translation exercises further the universality of Shakespeare's plays and show that different media can help illustrate the gist of a scene or a character. Websites such

Figure 10.4 *Macbeth* in Emojis. *Source*: Author's compilation.

Digital Methods and Visual Essays   141

Figure 10.5   **Tybalt on Twitter.** *Source*: The Cambridge Blog (April 23, 2014).

Figure 10.6   **Romeo and Juliet texting.** *Source*: The Cambridge Blog (April 23, 2014).

as ifaketextmessage.com or simitator.com are tools that create this digital content easily and efficiently. Moreover, translating text into digital content makes both the written text and the digital medium more accessible and comprehensible.

While our previous examples focused primarily on the written text that can be translated into different media, this of course also holds true for the medium of film. In an academic environment, in which the written text is usually preferred over the visual, let alone the audiovisual, film, even in the form of adaptations, is often neglected. However, by providing filmic adaptations of, for example, Shakespeare plays, various perspectives on the written word can be gained through a director's audiovisual interpretation.

Components such as costumes, mise-en-scène, camera angles, color schemes, and sound and music are means of highlighting certain aspects of a text. Moreover, it is often expedient to look at several film adaptations of the same text, since similarities and differences can be observed and intertextual or rather intermedial references can be discerned. Usually the films not only quote the play they are adapting but also each other.

Through this repetition, conclusions can be drawn about the various historical contexts of the film adaptations and about the visual imaginary culture created through these adaptations. This means that by perpetually emphasizing a particular aspect of a play in different film versions, the play becomes part of a culture that has its own dynamic when it comes to perceiving the text.

Creating digital content with the films and their still images can also highlight cultural aspects. The visuals can be used in relation to social media by means of gifs and memes. Scenes can be turned into gifs and stills into memes by adding a textual component. This enables students and teachers alike to engage with film material in a creative way, examine the imagery of the film closely, and think about both film and text critically.

Of course, memes and gifs can also be created by unrelated images that are then linked to the original text by association through the content presented in the meme. Thus, the famous meme that uses Boromir's quotation from the first movie of *The Lord of the Rings* trilogy, "One does not simply walk into Mordor," could be superimposed on a reference to *Macbeth*, "One does not simply ignore a prophecy," or to *Romeo and Juliet*, drawing out the irony of Romeo's swift exchange of love objects, "One does not simply fall in love." The image could still be that of Boromir but interlinking it with Shakespeare by means of content.

Of course, these statements could also be superimposed on a still image or a scene from a film adaptation of *Macbeth* or *Romeo and Juliet*. This playful engagement with films, texts, and content can then be further elaborated by extending it to a more in-depth analysis of the respective play through visual means.

DIGITAL DISCUSSIONS

Using the aforementioned digital methods to understand texts through visual culture, be it images, films, memes, or gifs, prepares not only for a visual analysis of the text but also introduces various techniques related to working with visual material, as the pictures must be found and put into context. This is especially useful when exploring alternative learning techniques, as Benedek observes: "In the past 25 years, several theorists [have] pointed out that increasing curricular requirements cannot be efficiently managed by formal education and the traditional tools of education should be modernised" (2016, 162).

Thus these abovementioned exercises allow for an essayistic approach to the work in question, as they highlight the subjective interpretation of a text. With this preparatory work in mind, we now comment on the use of essays in their traditional and their digital forms by discussing the idea of visual essays.

VISUAL ESSAYS

While John Conomos states that, "[f]or Montaigne, the essay was an ideal vehicle for speculating aloud and testing ideas on paramount questions of life, culture, politics, human fragility and society" (2016, 90), the essay in a university setting is thought to provide an objective analysis and interpretation of a text. Of course, interpretations are in themselves quite subjective, which is why Montaigne remains relevant to essay writing.

Moreover, while speculation is often avoided when critically engaging with texts, the testing of ideas through theses and arguments still plays an important role in the liberal arts. In discussing the subjective perspective, Laura Rascaroli explains that an essay is always personal, since it only offers the author's point of view:

> An essay is the expression of a personal, critical reflection on a problem or set of problems. Such reflection does not propose itself as anonymous or collective, but as originating from a single authorial voice.... This authorial "voice" approaches the subject matter not in order to present a factual report (the field of traditional documentary), but to offer an in-depth, personal, and thought-provoking reflection. (Rascaroli 2008, 35)

This "thought-provoking reflection" does not necessarily have to be expressed in written form. It can also be a visual exploration of topics that require reflection and discussion.

While literature studies in particular focus on the written word in terms of essays, film studies have developed the essay film to express an analytical engagement with general "problems," to use Rascaroli's word, by translating them into the medium of film. This is especially useful because essay films, as a genre, have "the ability to compress together, in a non-systematic fashion, such devices as collage, irony, pastiche, satire, humour and paradox" (Conomos 2016, 90).

In essay films, we thus find a playful compilation of rhetorical devices via images in order to present a critical thought process. In doing so, the essay film crosses boundaries between fact and fiction, since it is neither a mere presentation of knowledge, as it can often be found in documentaries, nor a fictional construct (cf. Rascaroli 2008, 24). In that respect, the essay film shares similarities with the literary essay, as Pantenburg (2015, 136) and Rascaroli explain.

In Rascaroli's assessment, "Transgression is a characteristic that the essay film shares with the literary essay, which is also often described as a protean form. The two foremost theorists of the essay are, as is well known, Theodor Adorno and Georg Lukács; both describe it as indeterminate, open, and, ultimately, indefinable." (Rascaroli 2008, 25)

This transgressive potential is why it makes sense to combine film studies and literary studies in order to create an essay that shares characteristics of both essay film and literary essay. Thus, "not bound to a specific genre, the essay appears as a strategic equivalent to modern thought. Only with the essay and its procedures, according to the tacit assumption, does modern thinking come about" (Pantenburg 2015, 138).

Both literary and film essays, therefore, have a similar structure with which to present this concept of modern thought; they both create an active dialogue between the text and its audience, as "each spectator, as an individual and not as a member of an anonymous, collective audience, is called upon to engage in a dialogical relationship with the enunciator, to become active, intellectually and emotionally, and interact with the text" (Rascaroli 2008, 36). It is the transgressive nature of both forms of essays and their dialogical structure that form the basis for a new kind of essay writing: the visual essay.

The visual essay can be defined as a digital analysis of textual and visual material that is combined into a critical argument. It presents an argument by means of combining images and/or film clips and text into an essayistic digital narrative. That is why the exploration of digital methods, such as social media approaches and poster-design sessions, is an important part in the process of acquiring the necessary skills to work with digital and visual material.

Using digital media allows students to engage more with visual patterns and narratives, thus offering new possibilities for critical discussions (cf. Benedek 2016, 162). A visual essay, like the literary essay and the film essay, is a hybrid of scientific research and artistic expression, where

> significant, meaningful elements in the work of art are brought together. At first, we quite simply start by looking at what is represented in the pictures, and how they are presented to us. This act of looking almost inevitably turns these images into a sequence, an argument. (Roes and Pint 2017, 3)

Roes and Pint's argument that seeing triggers thinking is especially relevant when we examine film adaptations of literary works.

Here, the film cuts, expands, and twists its referential template by shortening the story, by adding other components such as sounds, and by altering characters and even sometimes events. The adaptation can thus be seen as an interpretation of its parent-text that invites us to interpret it even further (cf. Straumann 2015). The visual essay does exactly that; it takes the adaptation or adaptations and discusses them as a medium of its own and then sets it in relation to the original text.

In this, the adaptation is neither judged nor evaluated by comparing it to the parent-text in terms of quality or accuracy. Instead, what is of interest is how the parent-text has been interpreted and what interested the screenwriter and director. In that way, "a visual essay can function as a tool for disclosing/articulating/communicating the kind of embodied thinking that occurs within an artistic practice or practice-based research" (Roes and Pint 2017, 3).

In order to create a visual essay, scenes are cut from films and rearranged into sequences through a collection of scenes that substantiate a claim to be made. This claim must also be included in the visual essay in order to make it stand on its own as a visual argument. While images can also speak for themselves in terms of argumentation, it is more helpful to include slides in-between images or film sequences, or to superimpose text onto them in order to present secondary research material.

This can also be done with a voice-over that leads the viewer through the argumentation process. In order to create a completed and engaging analysis, the use of sound and music can also be an advantage. Roes and Pint add that "the images also invite us to explore certain formal and compositional elements that keep recurring" (2017, 5). These elements form patterns that can be compared and contrasted through the sequencing of images. Therefore, a visual essay comprises visual, textual, and aural components that present a critical claim and academic argument.

CHALLENGES OF DIGITAL METHODS

The advantage of the visual essay over the traditional essay is therefore that the visual essay allows a comparison of film scenes and patterns directly, without the translation into text. The reader can see immediately what the argument tries to establish and describe, as

> Images are the expression of our on-going, complex relation with an inner and outer environment. In the process of making images of our environment, different bodily experiences, like affects, emotions, feelings and movements are mobilized in the creation of meaning. (Roes and Pint 2017, 2)

Since the visual essay not only incorporates images but also affects aural senses, it offers an analysis of different features of adaptations through a better representation of sound and music. Moreover, the subjective essayistic characteristic of the visual essay can be emphasized by adding another musical layer that is not part of the parent-text or adaptation but that is extra-diegetic and chosen for the analysis in order to substantiate and expand its arguments.

However, the visual essay also poses challenges that must be addressed, especially in a university environment. When students are confronted with the task of cutting a film and editing it into a new audiovisual creation, the task can often be overwhelming if they have not had any training. Since the schedule and budget often do not allow for tutorials or accompanying technical courses, students must acquire their skills using alternative tools.

While the digital methods described earlier are supposed to facilitate the use of technology, editing films requires a different skill set. In my own courses, I have found that the best way to introduce film editing into the classroom is through software and YouTube tutorials. Whether an advanced student takes over as a tutor and walks the students through the software step by step or the students work together in groups and watch YouTube tutorials is a matter of convenience as well as budget.

If the former option is chosen, the software must be set beforehand so that the students can watch the relevant tutorials. While there are many excellent premium programs, there are also a number of gratis open-access software options. An example for Windows would be Lightworks, while iMovie can be used for iOS devices. Both programs enable the simple editing of movies without the individual being proficient in film editing.

Another problem that occurs with regard to film editing is acquiring the films in a digital format. Here, the university needs to provide programs that allow the ripping of DVDs for internal university purposes. The instructor can then rip the DVDs and allow the students to use them, as long as they sign legal agreements confirming the material will only be used in the classroom and not distributed or used for private purposes. Of course, the films can also be downloaded if the specific country permits it. The best way to avoid legal issues is to get in touch with the university's legal department and discuss the legal obstacles that must overcome despite the wide distribution and use of digital content.

An additional challenge at the content level is the evaluation of visual essays. It is often difficult to consider the visual essay as a stand-alone unit that works for a comprehensive analysis. While a literary essay consists only of text, the visual essay also hints at the need for words even in a visual context. Phillip Lopate makes a plea for including textual components, suggesting that

> An essay-film must have words, in the form of a text either spoken, subtitled, or intertitled. Say all you like about visualization being at the core of thinking, I cannot accept an utterly pure, silent flow of images as constituting essayistic discourse. (Lopate, "In Search of the Centaur," 245; qtd. in Pantenburg 2015, 145)

This is why the visual essay should be accompanied by words in the form of a brief paper explaining the author's—which is to say, the student's—thought process and also presenting the argument in a textual form. Combining both paper and visual essay will result in a creative digital approach to analyzing and discussing audiovisual material.

CONCLUSION

The visual essay is a creative approach to exploring texts in all kinds of forms, be they written text, verbal text, film, or images. It enables us to illustrate patterns more directly and argue without having to mediate examples through text. The rearranging of film scenes into sequences thus allows a direct quotation of the film material and, as a consequence, a visual argument.

Nonetheless, the critical discussion must be supported and complemented by a textual component, as it makes an understanding of the visual presentation more accessible. While technical skills often pose a challenge to students, the preparation by means of digital methods in terms of intermedial approaches already establishes the basis for the final film editing the visual essay requires.

Despite the many obstacles, the visual essay, just like the essay film, "is a reaction to visual deficits; it attempts to rectify the muteness of the image by adding sound and thus guide the viewer's visual perception" (Pantenburg 2015, 145). In terms of visual essays, this muteness is not only overcome by the sound that can be added to the essay, but also by means of the critical narrative that is created in the sequencing of images, film scenes, and text. Thus, in the end, it is the analytical engagement with texts in an intermedial progress that constitutes the visual essay.

Chapter 11

Structural Shifts and the Graduate Literary Essay

Examples for the Twenty-First-Century Classroom

Shanthini Pillai

The horizon of literary studies in the twenty-first century has moved beyond traditional borders, especially when one considers that not many literary graduate students fall back onto the traditional career path of the hallowed halls of academic scholarship. In *Other Asias*, Gayatri Chakravorty Spivak speaks of the need to engage with the pedagogy of the humanities, as it revolves around "a more textured kind of work, entering through friendship with the language(s)," and states that the best platform to implement such a pedagogy is in the classroom, through "language-based close-reading laced with social scientific rigor" (Spivak 2008, 226).

While the intricacies of language and its social contexts are an ever-present mode of investigation, today's humanities classroom now integrates the multimodal complexities of the present age, and resting at its core is the digital network. This chapter focuses on new forms of the essay in the graduate literary classroom that can open up new frontiers for graduates who are interested in the field of literary studies but who wish to venture beyond the world of academe.

It will provide insights into developing the multimodal essay in the form of comprehensive digital productions that incorporate audiovisual aspects while maintaining the core of nuanced readings of cultural texts. In this way, this chapter engages with the expanding structural shift that Spivak writes about by providing ways to guide graduate students to present their interpretative responses to traditional printed literary texts through developing and designing multimodal essays that integrate diverse methods of meaning-making.

The premise of traditional classroom pedagogy is the unilateral transfer of knowledge from teacher to student. Since the advent of the millennium, teaching practices have shifted in emphasis from teacher to student, and this is especially evident in the way teachers have expanded the curriculum to accommodate multimodal texts in addition to more traditional book-based materials. Such a curriculum reflects a more pragmatic approach to learning and teaching, whereby the teaching of and learning about a particular area of study is couched in real-world situations and presented to the learner via various modals that can lead toward higher-order critical skills and help students make connections between textbook information and real-world phenomena.

Arthur Lewis and David Smith (1993) traced the evolution of the concept of critical thinking and linked it with problem-solving skills. They differentiated higher-order thinking and critical thinking by proposing that higher-order thinking encompasses "problem solving, critical thinking, creative thinking, and decision making" (136). To this end, they consider higher-order thinking as occurring when a person integrates or interrelates new information with stored information to generate possibilities in a given situation.

Literary studies has always prided itself on the inculcation of higher-order thinking skills, based on the premise that critical reading skills are instilled through immersion in the aesthetics of literary language. Thus, the traditional curriculum of an English Studies degree has always been weighed heavily in favor of the nuanced study of literary texts, with the inculcation of equally nuanced modes of both reading and writing. The assumption has always been that graduates would ultimately enter academe, especially upon gaining a graduate degree.

The conventional setting for teaching and learning in the graduate literary studies classroom has been the seminar, with its in-depth discussions of critical literary theories and diverse sociocultural issues and of tropics at an advanced level. Consequently, assessment techniques have been largely based on the seminar essay. The form of the essay in the English classroom has its roots in the works of Montaigne, Johnson, and Woolf, and the expectations of the final product of a graduate student seminar is that essays should mirror, where possible, the nuanced writing style of this literary genre.

Like the father of the essay, Montaigne, students should convey "with unexampled frankness" what their "opinion was about men and things" and throw "what must have been a strange kind of new light on many matters but darkly understood" (Hazlitt). In the words of Samuel Johnson, the student ought to be adept in "setting up a general assertion to be examined meticulously and in detail, challenging it from various points of view, and finally—having either accepted or rejected it—attempting to provide the result with some universal significance or application" (Spector 1997, 2).

Lastly, and keeping in mind that they write from within a literary context, their essay should, in the words of Virginia Woolf,

> lay us under a spell with its first word, and we should only wake, refreshed, with its last. In the interval we may pass through the most various experiences of amusement, surprise, interest, indignation. . . . The essay must lap us about and draw its curtain across the world. (2002, 120)

Thus, the literary essay should create an impact through powerful descriptive writing, mesmerize us with its creative power of reasoning, and convince us by the power of argument, while also, as Woolf cautions, avoiding overt ornamentation lest meaning be obfuscated.

These skills remain the core requirements of the seminar essay far into today's literary classroom. The seminar essay can be loosely defined as the transformation, into written form, of ideas that are discussed, with guidance from an educator, in the style of a forum within a graduate classroom (Andrews 2007, 4), and presented in ten to fifteen pages in traditional essay format. However, the contemporary graduate literature classroom exists in a world that is increasingly multidimensional, especially given progressive technology.

As such, educators are now faced with a multidimensional humanities pedagogy that must integrate the digital network, not only in modes of teaching but also in learning outcomes, both in the undergraduate and graduate classroom. The essay, too, must adapt to changing times. One of the ways in which the textures of humanities pedagogy can be transformed is by integrating the "communicational ensemble" (Kress and Van Leeuwen) of the layers of multimodal meaning-making within the process of teaching and learning.

This ensemble, as Gunther Kress and Theo Van Leeuwen explain, "concentrates on two things: (1) the semiotic resources of communication, the modes and the media used, and (2) the communicative practices in which these resources are used" (Kress and Van Leeuwen 2001, 111). All these different modes of instruments of communication, when arranged symmetrically, can work in unison to produce a single composition. When students are encouraged to use multimodal texts to convey meaning or articulate their interpretation of events or readings, they essentially acquire agency in the communicative process, as they become involved in the process of designing and transforming word to image and other modes as relevant (Kress 2003).

This aspect opens up an entire platform for the acquisition of literacies, as students are not hemmed in by the sole source, no matter how textured, of language. Once multimodality is incorporated into the learning process, the advancement of learning across different spaces can occur. When students are given a number of modes within which to communicate their ideas and articulate their interpretations, these in turn create portals for the reinvention of traditional pedagogical boundaries as they meet and engage with various disciplines.

This chapter presents a discussion of the structural shifts to the form of the traditional seminar essay as it is adapted to suit graduate contexts within a more multidimensional form, without losing sight of the basic tenets of the descriptive content of Montaigne, Johnson, and Woolf. It does so through a more "textured" pedagogical approach to the humanities that engages "language-based close-reading laced with social scientific rigor" (Spivak 2008, 226).

While the intricacies of language and its social contexts are an ever-present mode of investigation, shifting the dimension of the essay in the graduate literary classroom opens up new frontiers for graduates to engage with academia and beyond. An integral part of this process involves developing the multimodal essay in the form of comprehensive digital productions that incorporate audiovisual aspects while maintaining the core of nuanced readings of cultural texts.

In this way, the discussion engages with the expanding structural shift that Spivak speaks of by providing ways to guide graduates to present their interpretative responses to traditional printed literary texts through developing and designing multimodal essays that integrate diverse methods of meaning-making. It is also aware that contemporary literature classrooms are now more "literary–cultural" than purely literary, in line with ensuring sustainability amid the shifting grounds of electronic capitalism (Spivak 2012, 2).

Such modes of capitalism have inevitably led to an overemphasis on science and technology as the most sought-after disciplines in universities, and this has had drastic consequences for the humanities, considered more philosophical in nature and thus of less value in the commodification of higher education. Hence the humanities are put "under erasure" (Nelson 2011, 33) or, as Spivak phrases it rather bluntly but aptly, "the humanities and social sciences bite the dust" (Spivak 2012, 1).

Faced with this scenario, the literary graduate of today can find few prospects in academia, and even if interest and passion lead one to a literary graduate program, one does so fully aware that a literary studies degree may not necessarily lead to a university English department. This is especially applicable in the Asian context, where the sciences are valued above English, which, while certainly of value, is generally only at the proficiency level. Thus teaching-of-English degrees are more in demand than English degrees focusing primarily on literary studies.

As such, to ensure graduate marketability and employable relevance, the graduate literary degree must change with the times through structural shifts in both pedagogy and assessment. Academics in the humanities also face the pressure of staying relevant. Graduate literary programs in Malaysia are progressively adapting to these changes, resulting in some innovations in assessment modes. The discussion that follows provides samples from a master's program in Colonial and Postcolonial Literatures taught at the National University of Malaysia.

THE GRADUATE LITERARY ESSAY IN
THE MALAYSIAN CONTEXT

The Malaysian Qualifications Agency (MQA) is the body that oversees the best standards and practices of tertiary programs, both at the undergraduate and graduate levels in Malaysia. At the graduate level, assessment and learning outcomes are guided by the Bloom's taxonomy of learning objectives at the more advanced level, mainly level 4 of the affective domain and level 5 of both the cognitive and psychomotor domains.

As the essay is a form of assessment that mainly deals with the cognitive domain, essay-writing skills are mapped against the Structure of Observed Learning Outcome (SOLO) taxonomy developed by John B. Biggs and Kevin

F. Collis. These are reproduced in the MQA document, *Guidelines to Good Practices: Assessment of Students* (2014), and extracted below to present the range of assessment criteria used to differentiate a well-structured essay from a poorly structured essay and the range between the two.

Two levels of what is meant by a "well-structured essay" are first presented. At the most advanced level, it should have a "clear introduction and conclusion. Issues clearly identified; clear framework for organizing discussion; appropriate material selected. Evidence of wide reading from many sources. Clear evidence of sophisticated analysis or innovative thinking" (53).

One level below is an essay that is also well structured but that does not have the distinctive ability of sophisticated analysis or innovative thinking of the essay one level above it. At this level, the essay should present "a clear introduction and conclusion. Framework, which is well developed, exists. Appropriate material. Content has logical flow, with ideas clearly expressed. Clearly identifiable structure to the argument with discussion of differing views" (52). Thus at this level, the student should be able to present a level of argument that is able to differentiate among a variety of opinions.

At the third level is the essay that is *fairly well structured* and that reveals

> some issues identified. Attempt at a limited framework. Most of the material selected is appropriate. Introduction and conclusion exist. Logical presentation attempted and successful in a limited way. Some structure to the argument but only a limited number of differing views and no new ideas. (52)

Here, the essay lacks a level of critical argument, as surmised through the lack of reading and the inability to present new ideas. The premise for this category is that logic is impeded by a lack of critical argumentation skills, though it is still coherent.

At the fourth level is the essay that is poorly structured but has some saving attributes in that it shows that "a range of material has been selected and most of the material selected is appropriate." However, it presents a "weak introduction and conclusion" with "little attempt to provide a clear logical structure." It has a broad focus "on a large number of facts with little attempt at conceptual explanations," with "very little linking of material between sections" (53). As such, the essay at this level has few critical argumentation capabilities.

This is followed by the essay that has no saving grace whatsoever, in that it has "one issue identified and this becomes the sole focus." It reveals "no framework for organizing discussion" and proceeds only with a "dogmatic presentation of a single solution to the set task. This idea may be restated in different ways. Little support from the literature." In sum, at this level, the essay shows no element of critical selection, nor an accompanying dimension of critical argumentation.

The assessment of the traditional essay in the Malaysian graduate literary class often follows the process noted above, and the expectation of graduates is that they will be able to achieve at least the fourth level, with some critical argumentation skills. The ideal level is the first, with its evidence of "sophisticated analysis coupled with innovation," in line with the fifth level of the cognitive domain, to establish, assemble, and integrate key concepts through critical argumentation.

The intricacies of the critical dimension are crucial at the graduate level. As Richard Andrews (2007), in a study of assessments of British graduate academic writing, puts it, "critical thinking is the desired dialectical substratum; argumentation is the process by which such thinking is manifested; and argument is the finished product (the essay, the dissertation)" (2007, 3). Critical argumentation, he adds, will only be achieved when the entire work that is submitted shows that it has:

> (a) worked out its theoretical position, (b) reviewed the literature, (c) designed an appropriate empirical study (if it is that kind of study), (d) gathered the evidence, (e) arrayed the evidence into categories and (f) found its own position in relation to those categories, arranging them in a sequence that carries the argument of the piece as a whole. (12)

Yet, if we are to propel the humanities scholar into "innovation," the catchphrase of the posthuman world, the form of the essay must be expanded to shift its structures into a more multimodal form. It is here that the application of the four pedagogical processes of situated practice, overt instruction, critical framing, and transformed practice, as espoused by Cope and Kalantzis and the New London Group (Cope and Kalantzis 2005, 31), are useful in transforming the traditional textual essay into a multi-textured form. However, these are interwoven with fundamental critical argumentation through the knowledge processes of experiencing, conceptualizing, analyzing, and applying (Cope and Kalantzis 2015, 24) what has been learned.

The educator must constantly keep in focus that the ultimate aim of graduate literary education is to harness the advanced critical skills of analyzing, synthesizing, applying, and evaluating information from a set of reading materials. In the graduate literary classroom, these materials usually take the form of novels, poetry, and drama, although the classroom's literary–cultural amalgamation has increasingly led to the inclusion of film as a cultural narrative. The discussion below presents ways in which students in a graduate class became involved in the situated practices of designing their own form of interactive essay, as multimodal features are used to transform the traditional essay format.

TWENTY-FIRST-CENTURY FORMS OF THE SEMINAR ESSAY

In a graduate course centered on postcolonial theory and issues, students were guided into understanding the dialectics of Occidental–Oriental power relations using works by Edward Said, Homi Bhabha, and Gayatri Chakravorty Spivak. In seminar discussions, they began by discussing key theoretical concepts raised by these three theorists as presented in selected reference materials. Subsequently, through instruction and guided discussion, students proceeded to analyze selected literary texts containing representations of communities with a history of colonization, for example, Native Americans, Africans, and Indians. The selected texts were *The Life of P.T. Barnum* by P. T. Barnum (1855), *Heart of Darkness* by Joseph Conrad (1889), and a selection of stories from Rudyard Kipling's *Plain Tales from the Hill* (1888).

These representations were then mapped against the core theoretical concepts of Said's Orientalism, Bhabha's ambivalence, and Spivak's gendered subaltern. The desired learning outcome objective was that students would be able to produce critical argumentation through in-depth analysis of the aesthetic qualities of the literary texts by means of the careful and seamless integration of the key theoretical concepts learned. Following the seminar discussions, students' critical analytical skills were assessed through a series of evaluations.

The first evaluation was a preliminary theoretical seminar essay which entailed a critical review of the concepts learned in the first three seminar sessions which had focused on selections from the works of Said, Bhabha, and Spivak. Students were required to explain their understanding of the selected works by commenting on significant issues raised by the three postcolonial theorists. In order to do so, they were asked to provide relevant excerpts and critically discuss how these were connected to specific concepts.

The essay submitted was assessed according to its level of critical engagement based on the SOLO essay criteria outlined above. As such, this first assessment adhered to the traditional requirements of a graduate seminar essay. The second assessment, however, shifted the traditional structure of the seminar essay to more interactive grounds. In this assessment, students were asked to transfer the critical discussion of the three literary texts read during their graduate seminar sessions into a multimodal digital composition of the seminar essay. This digital product expanded the boundaries of the traditional form of written critical interpretation, as it shapeshifted into a more interactive element by incorporating hypertexts and other Web 2.0 features, thus literally bringing the essay (a)live.

The central focus of the assessment, however, did not stray from the traditional expectations of the graduate seminar essay. The end product had to show critical engagement with the three literary texts and evidence of key theoretical concepts, thus revealing students' ability to critically synthesize at a more advanced level. They were also asked to justify the proper application of key aspects of postcolonial theory and to demonstrate critical arguments on postcolonial issues in their textual analysis.

In a preparatory session of overt instruction, students were guided in the use of Google sites as a platform for developing their digital seminar essay. They were led to the Google sites page and prompted to follow the instructions presented on how to create a webpage using the site's webpage creation tools. As the Google sites webpage is user-friendly, complex technological know-how was not required. Students merely followed the self-explanatory instructions to create their digital composition. They were then instructed on the development of the content required for the website. The instructions followed the usual essay question format, with extra details on integrating multimodal, interactive digital elements.

Students were first asked to reflect on the fact that the seminar sessions had shown that nineteenth-century colonial literary narratives contained a set of distinctive features that presented the dialectics of power and subordination, as conceptualized and discussed at length by Said, Bhabha, and Spivak. Students were subsequently instructed to develop a digital essay in the form of a website that presented features of Orientalism in the *Life of P.T. Barnum*, the ambivalence of colonial discourse in *Heart of Darkness*, and the gendered subaltern in *Plain Tales from the Hills*.

These instructions followed the traditional essay question and outlined the traditional expectations of critical reflection, exploration, and argument. Students were reminded that, as with any seminar essay, the analysis of the texts should present the key elements of critical argumentation as outlined by Andrews above; that is, they should (a) map out the theoretical positions according to the respective theories, (b) present a review of the literature written on the literary texts in question, (c) critically organize the evidence that they had extracted from the literary texts into specific theoretical categories, and (d) present all of the above in a coherent and holistic manner evidencing their own position in relation to the entire argument.

Once these instructions were relayed, the students were then guided in how to transfer this traditional content of critical argument into a more multimodal form in the digital realm. It is here that the form of the twenty-first-century seminar essay begins to take shape. Firstly, students were asked to create a homepage introducing their website in a manner similar to the traditional introduction to a seminar essay.

At the end of the introduction, they were asked to present the three sections required of the seminar essay: Orientalism in Barnum, ambivalence in Conrad, and the gendered subaltern in Kipling. These three sections were to be hyperlinked to their own separate subpages, thus entering the world of hypertext. Each of the subpages would present a critical discussion of the three texts. This critical argument would be separated into sections of theoretical categories, also hyperlinked to their own pages.

Journeying further into the hypertext world, students were then asked to present their critical positions by selecting three theoretical categories from each of the theorists, complete with a discussion of how these categories are evident in the extracts from the literary texts. They were also instructed to present two accompanying visuals that would reflect the content in each subpage. These visuals should as far as possible correlate to the scene presented in the excerpt. As the webpages would be presented only to the class and within an educational framework, the pictures would adhere to fair use guidelines, as they would not be published in a public forum or in a journal article, where copyright issues would apply.

The final product would eventually reflect a digital portfolio on the colonial Americas, Africa, and India, taking the form of an online critical gallery, integrating visuals with supporting textual information. While the central focus was on critical discussions of Occidental–Oriental power relations, as evident in the analysis of the three texts selected, the structure of the webpages that were designed also required an element of critical digital curating. Students' selection of information from the literary texts, with the accompanying textual discussion of the material, would essentially take viewers through what were essentially online exhibition galleries on colonial Americas, Africa, and India.

Their critical discussion of the material, organized according to various postcolonial theoretical categories, transformed what would have been a unidimensional essay into a multidimensional corridor. Students were not only required to present their knowledge of the dialectical interplay of power and powers of representation within specific sociocultural contexts, but also to think of the strategic design and layout features of their webpage: color scheme, appropriate design, and font size were some of the issues they had to consider.

In this way, what would have been a traditional pedagogy taking students through a close textual study was reinvented to enable a more novel approach to a critical engagement with Occidental concepts and how to present them in an innovative manner. The seminar essay traveled through and was transformed by a portal that gave it twenty-first-century features of hypertextuality. As Carey Jewitt notes,

> seeing the communicational landscape of the classroom through a multimodal lens has significant implications for conceptions and processes of learning. Thinking about learning as a process of design and choice of representation gives a renewed focus on the role of the learner. Design, diversity, and multiplicity emphasise the meaning-making practices and interpretative work of students. (258)

As the literature classroom expands its horizons, increasingly complex ideas can be explored through various combinations of analysis, application, synthesis, and evaluation, as revealed in the sample of the transformed graduate seminar essay presented in this chapter. Such innovative strategies are absolutely crucial in classroom settings that are no longer monomodal or unidimensional. Through such multimodal environments, both educators and students can be made aware of the vast resources available from literary studies and thus forge a way toward an optimum transfer of knowledge in the graduate classroom.

Other assessments in a range of courses convened over the years have similarly experienced reinventions of traditional literary studies that result in shifting disciplinary boundaries. For instance, in another graduate literary course that emphasized the role of literary studies in the real world, students were required to study contemporary Malaysian songs and music and to produce a research paper discussing evidence of multicultural engagement. The assessment rubrics required them to present a knowledge of multiculturalism in its general context as well as in the Malaysian context, followed by a review of multiculturalism in global popular music and Malaysian popular music.

Students were subsequently asked to present an analysis of a selected Malaysian popular music video that reflected an engagement with multiculturalism. The reports that were submitted for assessment revealed the ability of the students to conduct in-depth research into the history of the Malaysian popular music industry, reaching as far back as the 1960s. They produced reviews of the visuals of album covers and discussed the ways in which the music industry showed a progression from the Occidentalist influence of British bands in the early 1960s to the rising awareness of Asian identity in the late 1960s and the advent of Malaysian identity and nationhood in the 1970s and 1980s.

The students also drew connections with similar trends in the rise of postcolonial literary history and raised interesting points about the different depictions of and engagement with multiculturalism in the country, especially with regard to class and gender. In another topic, students were guided into recognizing literary elements in real-world products. This entailed paying attention to the interaction of visual and verbal elements in commercial products and their advertisements, with a particular focus on the ways in which the language used in the products was linked to the visuals.

Students were taught to think about the use of specific words, phrases, and connotations and to determine their corresponding elements in the visuals. They were also directed to make connections with critical issues, such as cultural identity, gendered discourse, the centering or marginalization of cultures, and exotification, among others. In this way, as with the other projects discussed above, the significance of core literary concepts and the tools of analysis were seen as crucial elements enabling higher critical awareness in the commercial sector.

The assessment required students to present a particular product and reveal how literary elements were used by the company in question to persuade customers to buy that product. The presentations revealed interesting aspects related to the use of persuasive cultural ideology, the semiotics of Orientalism, cultural symbols, dramatic impact, and globalization and class. These were discussed in relation to such products as confections, automobiles, sports shoes, and beverages. As in the other course assessments presented above, disciplinary boundaries were made malleable by integrating core literary precepts. However, the assessments always included one traditional seminar essay to ensure that critical skills of argumentation remained at the core of the syllabus.

What the discussion has shown is that the horizon of literary studies has evolved and expanded, especially when one considers that few literary graduates in Asia can fall back on the traditional career path of becoming academic scholars. The shifts in the structure of the literary seminar essay discussed above can be a way of making viable a discipline that many, in Asia especially, feel is only relevant within the realm of education. This leads one to consider ways in which new frontiers can be created for graduates who are interested in the field of literary studies but who wish to venture beyond the world of academe. Pedagogical reinventions such as those discussed above can be crucial in emphasizing the validity of literary studies and its multifold textures that promote critical meaning-making in the larger scheme of educational progress in Asia.

Chapter 12

Not for Everyone
Experiments in Assessment
Kevin A. Morrison

Graduate-level seminars often have two goals. The first is intellectual. They are intended to orient students to a particular set of texts in keeping with the defined historical or thematic parameters of the syllabus. A student enrolled in Renaissance Literature should expect to gain foundational knowledge of the array and breadth of literary works written in this era. By contrast, one who elects to take, say, Trauma in Literature will be prepared to focus on narrative techniques and representational strategies while studying a variety of filmic, televisual, fictional, and nonfictional texts.

The second goal of graduate-level seminars is professional. While graduate coursework helps familiarize students with the discipline and its research methodologies, individual seminars often aid those who have enrolled in their transition from being students to becoming junior members of the profession. A seminar on Romanticism will include PhD students intending to specialize in this area and preparing for comprehensive examinations, a dissertation, and a subsequent career. It will also include students from other literary fields who are fulfilling distribution requirements in order to gain the breadth of literary, cultural, and historical knowledge necessary to profess literature.

However, many graduate seminars will likely serve a far more diverse population. Some literature departments have eliminated terminal MA programs, choosing to award the degree as students progress to the PhD. At the same time, many universities have recognized the potential of terminal degree programs for revenue generation. Some literary studies graduate seminars, therefore, attract students who are enrolled in broadly conceived MA programs: the humanities, the liberal arts, and interdisciplinary studies.

These programs do not typically maintain their own faculty lines. Although the requirements of these MA programs may include a foundational course, often referred to as a "core," which is designed to orient matriculants to humanistic study, students usually obtain their degree by taking a number of electives and, in some cases, completing a thesis. Students in these programs, therefore, add to existing department courses and often bolster enrollments of seminars. Although some universities share the revenues derived from these programs with the departments providing instruction and thesis supervision, this is not universally the case (ADE 2011).

Nevertheless, many literature departments have welcomed the additional bodies in the classroom. Shrinking admissions in graduate programs—reflecting institutional budget constraints that have curtailed the number of fellowships awarded as well as the precipitous decline in the availability of tenure-track jobs—has led to a rethinking of the seminar, a fundamental element of American postbaccalaureate education. In order to ensure that seminars remain institutionally viable, many literature departments have themselves begun to cast wider nets. These efforts include opening seminars to advanced undergraduates and graduate students from cognate disciplines and in cross-listing seminars with relevant departments.

As a result, graduate seminars now routinely include students whose backgrounds or motivations fundamentally differ from those of PhD students in literary studies. A seminar in literature may include doctoral students in history, art history, or philosophy who are interested in the period or topic but whose disciplinary norms and forms of writing will vary. A seminar may also include students in the aforementioned broad-based MA programs. Some will aspire to enter PhD programs. Others will hope to secure teaching positions at private high schools or at junior or community colleges and have little predilection for research.

Seminars also increasingly include third- and fourth-year undergraduates and honors students. Although there are certainly exceptions, undergraduate students, more often than not, complete assignments for the sake of a grade. Instead of being driven by intellectual curiosity or drawing on prior knowledge as context for new discovery, students tend to take an assigned essay prompt and transform it into the main argument of their essays.

By contrast, PhD students are expected to be deeply self-motivated, driven to hone their understanding of and capacity for literary criticism, capable of performing original thought, and adept at (or showing the potential for) conceptual self-reflexivity. This includes being able to locate oneself intellectually, articulating the theoretical premises of one's argument and defining the important terms. With the undergraduate student at one end of the spectrum and the doctoral student at the other, the MA student may fall somewhere in the middle.

Given this diverse population, is the seminar paper uniformly the right instrument of assessment? This chapter draws on the author's experiences of providing students with the option to choose from among several assessment packages.[1] It outlines the elements of these packages and the rationales behind them and incorporates anonymous reflective commentary by students about their experiences. It concludes with an appraisal of the difficulties in and possibilities of enabling students to select assignments that cultivate or refine different skills according to their professional aspirations and individual motivations.

OPTIONS FOR ASSESSMENT

For many graduate seminars, the final essay is the most significant learning project of the semester. Providing students with a vast scope for freedom within the general confines of the themes and issues of a seminar, the essay assignment enables, and indeed requires, them to synthesize theories, techniques, and methods in individuated ways. As Philip Robinson-Self argues elsewhere in this volume, the essay remains the signature pedagogy of the discipline of literary studies. Nevertheless, in order to accommodate the increasingly diverse population of the graduate seminar, it may be desirable to offer a range of assessment options.

Certainly, all students should be expected to attend seminars regularly and make lively, informed, critical, and respectful contributions to discussions. But the bulk of one's seminar grade could depend on different combinations of elements selected by that individual. One of the advantages of providing students with assessment options is that it enables them to play a cooperative role in determining the measures by which they will be evaluated.

By providing students with opportunities to choose their own forms of assessment, professors broaden the basis for active learning. Although active learning tends to be associated with in-class activities, such as small group work that—through engagement with research questions—generates critical thinking, it encompasses any effort to have students take responsibility for their seminar or course performance. Among the many benefits of active learning is enhanced motivation (Prince 2004; Anderson 2016, 11–24).

Of course, all forms of assessment should motivate student learning. As Philip Race, Sally Brown, and Brenda Smith have argued, "Assessment should allow students to self-assess and monitor their progress throughout a course, and help them make informed choices about what to learn, how to learn it, and how best to evidence the achievement of their learning" (2005, 3). If students are called on to play a role in formulating the terms of their own assessment, they are placed in the position of having to make conscious choices about how they will obtain and utilize knowledge.[2]

Moreover, students who have made a decision about how they will be assessed are likely to see the seminar as more distinctly tied to their individual goals. "Having a choice between assessment options," one student remarked, "was helpful to me because I was able to select the particular skills I wanted a chance to improve on." For example, those whose academic careers do not currently project entry into a PhD program (such as MA students or undergraduates) may favor skills-based forms of assessment. By contrast, doctoral students may wish to focus on developing and complicating their arguments and analyses.

This cohort was given the option of choosing one of two assessment packages:

Package 1:
- Facilitating seminar discussion twice
- Writing two 8-page papers on separate topics
- Integrating these two papers into a final project of 20–25 pages

Package 2:
- Facilitating seminar discussion once and conducting a teaching or research presentation
- Workshopping a 250-word abstract of the seminar essay
- Completing a final paper of 20–25 pages

The responsibility for facilitating discussion is a fixed element of both packages. However, it is weighted differently depending on whether a student opts to write a final paper in stages (package one) or during a single, intensive period (package two).

When conducted well, discussions can be immensely beneficial to both the individual facilitating them and the participants. Yet, as Barbara Gross Davis has noted, "[i]nitiating and sustaining a lively, productive discussion are among the most challenging of activities for an instructor" (1993, 63). By formalizing the responsibility for facilitating discussion as an element of assessment, students must necessarily reflect on the importance of "essential questions"—those that are thought provoking, open ended, and engaging (McTighe and Wiggins 2013, 3).

Questions are, of course, a vital element of research as well. With these options, students can choose between conceptualizing a single research question, capacious enough to be explored in a 20–25-page paper or two research questions explored in separate assignments. Those who choose the second option must initially articulate their question in a 250-word abstract and refine and develop it over the course of writing and revising a 20–25-page paper.

Students who choose the second package are also required to give a teaching or a research presentation. For those contemplating a career in academia, these presentations can be helpful preparation for campus visits. At research-focused universities, a presentation of one's dissertation is a necessary element of the job interview. At teaching-intensive universities and liberal arts colleges, job candidates are often expected to instruct an assembled group of faculty and graduate students on a short work that they read in advance.

Instead of a research or a teaching presentation, students who select the first option are charged with leading discussion twice. Depending on the course, students may be asked to facilitate a conversation on, first, a set of historical materials and, second, scholarly articles or a research monograph. The second assignment enables students to become adept at thinking about literature in relation to its historical context and increasingly comfortable with summarizing and critiquing extant scholarly work.

In terms of their written work, students who opt for the first package confront more modest tasks. They are to ask and answer two different questions within the span of conference-length papers. After these two assignments are completed, however, they must formulate a broader question that links and integrates the two essays into a final project. This additional responsibility is intended to help them hone their skills of comparative analysis.

Students who have undertaken this assignment have often expressed their appreciation for the opportunity. "I found the shorter papers to be a really valuable exercise because they forced me to dig deep and be concise (something I struggle with)," said one PhD student. Nevertheless, to this person the assignment appeared deceptively simple: "I do think it should be emphasized perhaps a bit more what sorts of struggles one might face in combining papers." The challenge was not to write each stand-alone paper but instead to justify the basis for and undertake the task of comparison.

Other students, however, acknowledged that the responsibility of having to write two papers before combining them helped them to be engaged in research and writing throughout the term. "Working with a subject from the beginning of the semester," observed another doctoral student, "helped me in developing my final paper more fully than simply starting research at the end of the semester." For this person, the key to making the assignment successful was to have in mind a working hypothesis—before writing the second paper—that linked the texts explored in otherwise separate essays.

An MA student who selected the first package appreciated the mix of elements that constituted the basis for assessment. "I feel confident speaking and in facilitating," this person wrote, "and I want to learn how to write. When the product (single final paper) is valued rather than the process (of learning how to write), I lose the impetus to do well." Sally Brown and Peter Knight have contended that diverse forms of assessment are necessary to ensure that no particular kind of learner is privileged (1994, 7). Intriguingly, this student's comment directly links multiple methods of assessment to increased motivation.

A doctoral student who chose the second package was eager to develop a complex argument. This person found great utility in "being forced to articulate my thinking about the texts (and therefore to also think about my writing) during the semester." Although not by course design, this student found that the research presentation early in the semester had laid the groundwork for the abstract, which was workshopped among peers on two occasions, and the final paper. The student expressed confidence that the submitted essay was well beyond what could have been accomplished if the assignment had been left to the end of the term.

SEQUENCED ASSIGNMENTS

Any number of other permutations is possible. One approach that can be particularly effective is sequenced assignments. Janet Auten's contribution to this volume discusses the seminar essay as the culminating project of an assignment sequence: from the response journal, in which students observe textual details and record initial ideas, to an annotated bibliography, in which students begin to critically analyze the work of other scholars, to the researched essay, which is directly informed by the tasks that preceded it.

This method breaks down the writing of a research essay into a series of manageable steps. It, therefore, teaches students how to tackle scholarly projects of considerable length. Although the above example from package one is not strictly speaking sequential, insofar as students write two self-contained essays before employing a comparative approach, it also, nevertheless, trains students to think of a longer project as comprised of smaller sections. It encourages them to see each 8–10-page paper as a section of a more extended, comparative inquiry.

Instead of developing a kernel of an idea in stages, as in the above example, students could also cultivate a particular set of skills through sequenced assignments. The cultivation of these abilities is accomplished by assigning three essays of increasing complexity that build on each other. Thus, sequencing may also consist of stand-alone, predominantly skills-based (rather than content-based), assignments:

- Close reading of a single passage (the first essay)
- Close reading of an entire text but rooted in a single passage (the second essay)
- Comparative textual analysis rooted in select passages from two works (third essay)

For some students, a series of assignments spread evenly throughout the semester may be more valuable than a single summative project. Indeed, this approach is more akin to forms of continuous assessment with which many are familiar from their years as undergraduates.

The first essay asks students to undertake an analytical exposition of a specific passage from a given work. While paying close attention to such details as grammar, vocabulary, figures of speech, literary devices, tone, and style, students unpack the argument or main point of a single passage. Although close reading is a foundational skill in literary analysis, most graduate students are eager to move from an analysis to a consideration of wider implications. They can find this exercise, therefore, surprisingly challenging.

Art historian Jennifer L. Roberts has written about the rewards of attending to a single painting for an excruciatingly long time. She ultimately noticed significant details that formed the basis of her interpretation. These details were not, however, at first immediately obvious to her: "Just because something is available instantly to vision does not mean that it is available instantly to consciousness" (2013, 42). Requiring a similarly decelerated and immersive approach, this initial essay assignment encourages developing patience as a skill.

In order to closely read, after all, one must keep contextualizing details—indeed, any particulars outside the specific passage under consideration—to a minimum. In Roberts's terms, such a method instills in one "the value of critical attention, patient investigation, and skepticism about immediate surface appearances" (42). This applies no less to literary studies than it does to art history.

The second essay assignment moves students into somewhat more familiar territory. They can be expected to undertake a close reading of a passage in the wider context of the work from which it is extracted. While the same stakes for close reading are present in this assignment, students are also responsible for linking a given passage to larger themes and currents. For example, what new problems or ideas, if any, does the passage raise? How does the passage advance ideas first articulated or developed in other chapters or sections? What is significant about this passage in terms of the text as a whole?

It may be tempting to have students continue working with the same passage that they selected for the first assignment. This would give them an additional opportunity to engage with what is likely to be—for the sake of a productive exercise—a conceptually and rhetorically difficult passage. It would also enable them to incorporate feedback before adding an additional layer of complexity to their analyses. However, since the seminar will have moved on from the readings and issues discussed earlier in the semester, when the first assignment is due, it can be more profitable to link the second essay to a new cluster of texts and topics.

The third writing assignment can build on the previous two and share the same expository, contextual, and argumentative stakes. In this assignment, however, students can be asked to closely read passages from two different works while at the same time giving critical attention to the potential connections or significant divergences between them. Their original argument, which puts these two texts in conversation, will stem from the analytic and contextual exposition of single passages. This assignment is intended to improve the students' capacity for textual comparison while further honing critical patience.

Sequenced assignments provide professors not only with several opportunities throughout the semester to assess student writing. They can also give them a number of occasions to gauge the level of student understanding of the seminar readings as well as their comprehension of the topics in which those readings are clustered. For students, the skills they gain or refine from undertaking a set of exercises are certainly transferable to settings where a single essay remains the only form of assessment utilized.

USING DIFFERENT PROFESSIONAL GENRES

For PhD students working in other historical periods or literatures than the one covered by a seminar, as well as advanced undergraduates and MA students who are contemplating an academic career, a different set of assignments may be in order. For them, the opportunity to further develop their capacity for writing in the shorter professional genres can be an attractive proposition.

Although the requirements of an academic job include diverse forms of writing, relatively few are actually taught. The remainder of this chapter will focus on two other possible assessment packages that introduce students to a broad array of genres:

Package 1:
- Facilitating seminar discussion twice
- Writing a 20–25-page final paper

Package 2:
- Facilitating seminar discussion once
- Writing a book review

- Writing an abstract for a conference paper
- Writing a grant or fellowship proposal
- Writing an 8–10-page conference paper or a critical note

With the same stakes for posing effective discussion questions as a common feature of both packages, the first option requires students to lead discussion twice and produce a lengthy, research-based essay. This may be developed in conversation with the instructor, but—for the most part—students pursue this activity on their own.

By contrast, students who opt for the second package are charged with using different genres of professional writing that are assessed at different stages over the course of an academic term. This package should give students a sense of range: from the book review to the conference paper abstract to the grant or fellowship proposal to the conference paper or critical note.

As conceptualized here, the series of assignments begins with a book review. Many academics stay current in their field by reading reviews of newly published works. Most journals include robust book reviews sections. Yet academics are generally biased against writing them (Eisenman 2002). Karen Kelsky, who provides academic consulting services targeted to graduate students and untenured PhDs, warns that book reviews may be "distracting you from writing the peer-reviewed publication that will actually count" (2015, 105). Yet there are many intellectually sound reasons for countering this assertion.

Reviews require that writers anticipate the questions that readers would have about a work and attempt to answer them. Part of a reviewer's job is to give readers an encapsulated picture of what the work is, in a factual way, with reference to its relevant qualities. A reviewer must, therefore, give a brief summary of the essential features of the work. A review will need to explain the work's central terminology while being relatively jargon-free itself. This gives readers a clear understanding of what is being reviewed. A reviewer will also want to remark on any unique organizational or structural features: for example, a collection of essays or a mode of writing that attempts to blend the discursive and the creative.

But one's remit as a reviewer goes further. At their best, book reviews do not simply summarize (Olnas and Leppälä 2013). They balance descriptive and evaluative elements. A reviewer, after all, must also assess a work's value as intellectual inquiry. This necessitates that a review has a thesis and a point of view, which in turn shapes the way the review is organized and developed. A review will, therefore, include value judgments, which tend to reflect the reviewer's own taste, judgment, and values, as one comments on a work's thesis, scope, methodology, significance, and stylistics. Insofar as book reviews are "evaluative commentaries" (Obeng-Odoom 2014, 79), they can act as a spur to professional growth.

Once students have written a review, which requires them to describe and evaluate the work of another, they might then be tasked with writing an abstract for a presentation. The abstract requires one to articulate—precisely and concisely—a contextualized thesis and to establish its importance and relevance. Because conference organizers usually select abstracts on the basis of their relevance to a conference theme, sometimes it is useful to have students select an event to which they can imagine submitting. But the goal of this exercise is ultimately skills-based, and, for those not intending to stay in academia, transferrable.

Conferences provide academics with opportunities to share their preliminary findings. The discussion that follows a presentation often shapes the subsequent trajectory of one's research. In writing an abstract, therefore, students need to be less concerned with the validity of their argument than with its coherence, plausibility, and interest. When these elements are emphasized, many students feel released from the pressure of having to prematurely master their topic.

Much like book reviews, abstract writing is not generally taught in the humanities. It can be helpful, therefore, to provide students with a number of prewriting exercises. For example, they might be asked to write a paragraph reflecting on how they got to their topic or on the problem or debate in the field to which the project addresses itself. Or they might be required to produce an outline that shows clearly how each section advances the paper's argument. Some of the sentences produced by these exercises might find their way into the abstract, but the primary purpose is to aid students in crystallizing their thoughts.

Although a logical next step might be to produce the conference paper itself, it can be equally valuable to have students undertake the writing of a grant or fellowship proposal. Working on the same project for which they wrote a conference paper abstract, students must present its rationale and importance in an entirely different way. The fellowship or grant proposal is longer than an abstract. Unlike conference organizers, many grant and fellowship reviewers are not specialists in one's field. Thus, students must learn how to write about their project in compelling but not field- or even disciplinary-specific terminology.

In writing a grant or fellowship proposal, students must necessarily give some thought to methodology and sources. Is this a historicist project that requires contextualizing archival work? Is it a work of textual criticism that necessitates consulting an original manuscript or versions of a manuscript? Is it a form of biographical inquiry that involves examining diaries, letters, or photographs? Such an exercise, therefore, can help them to determine their own intellectual self-location.

Students will also need to give thought to the kinds of financial support they require to further develop their project. This is usually reflected in a detailed and realistic budget that includes a summary and cost categories. Just as it can assist students in writing an abstract to have a particular call for papers in mind, it can be helpful for them to identify a specific grant agency or funding body for their project and to conform their proposal to its requirements. This will entail their spending time investigating the sources of funding that do exist, which itself can be a valuable exercise.

For the final assignment, students can be asked to write either a conference paper or a critical note. This provides an instructor with the opportunity to discuss both genres. Students should be encouraged to think of the conference paper as comprising the following elements:

- An introduction (250–300 words)
- Five to seven paragraphs
- A conclusion

Because students are to approach this assignment as if they were writing for an actual conference, they will need to pay careful attention to how the paper will be received by listeners.

Papers that are delivered orally should be written in pithy sentences with clear transitions and minimal quotation. Instead of a leisurely introduction, the first paragraph should contain and contextualize the thesis. In addition, it should offer clear signposts—a sense of how the argument will unfold—so that the listener will be able to follow the speaker's train of thought. The subsequent paragraphs and conclusion will follow the argumentative path laid out in the introduction.

Another possibility is to have students undertake the writing of a critical note. This assignment would necessitate students familiarizing themselves with the requirements of this genre and the journals that specialize in publishing them. For example, *Notes and Queries*, *ANQ*, *Explicator*, and *ELN* all specialize in publishing critical notes. Each journal's submission requirements and the types of articles they publish do, however, vary.

Indeed, despite commonalities among them, each of these journals has a different strength. *Notes and Queries* is concerned with the "asking and answering of readers' questions." *ANQ* specializes in essays of any length that uncover allusions, offer variant readings of manuscripts, or explicate sources. Whereas *Notes and Queries* and *ANQ* will publish essays on canonical and noncanonical literature, the *Explicator* focuses on frequently taught and anthologized works and privileges text-based criticism. All three are open to general submission. *ELN* only accepts manuscripts for theme-based issues.

For students whose primary field of specialization is not the focus of the course, the writing of a critical note can be a useful exercise that yields a potential publication. While a critical note cannot take the place of a journal article, it may be better than a seminar paper to which one will never return. This is precisely the outcome—as Gabriel Morrison and Thomas Deans show in their contribution to this volume—of many seminar papers. Because students are often writing substantial papers for seminars in fields that are not their own, it is often the case that once the task of writing is finished, students never again revisit the paper.

To write a critical note, a student must obtain mastery over a—admittedly far more narrow—subject matter and formulate a (comparatively modest) original argument. Yet a critical note does not require the extensive research that is necessarily a part of writing the seminar paper. Moreover, a critical note may provide students with an opportunity to try out a methodological approach with which they are unfamiliar. Finally, a critical note is manageable within the confines of an academic term.

CONCLUSION

For an instructor, one of the most challenging aspects of offering the option of assessment packages is the increased workload. Instead of devoting time at the end of the semester to reading a batch of essays, an instructor will be continuously engaged with (at least) some students' written work. Instructors can also expect increased email exchanges and in-person discussions with these students as the deadlines for each written assignment draw near.

The increased workload may to some extent be offset by other formalized responsibilities that are included in each assessment package. If students share the burden of facilitating discussion and are provided with opportunities to give teaching and research presentations as well as to workshop their abstracts or papers, some of the instructor's time is freed to focus on evaluating written work. The quality of writing and thinking by many students will, as a result of these engagements with their peers and instructors, improve as the term unfolds. Thus, the amount of time an instructor spends on assignments in the latter half of a term will likely be less than the time spent in the first half.

But the question of an instructor's workload is ultimately subsidiary to a larger consideration. In his study of the messiness of American graduate education today, Leonard Cassuto offered the following riposte to those whom, in his estimation, cling to outmoded understandings of the graduate seminar. He writes: "It's time—past time, really—to think about the seminar from the student's point of view as well as the teacher's" (2015, 67).[3] For Cassuto, graduate seminars should be reconceived: instead of emphasizing the learning of content, they should stress the acquisition of skills.

Where Cassuto proposes a skills-based approach to replace a content-driven model of graduate education, the experiments in assessment outlined in this chapter suggest an alternative. Instead of dispensing with content, instructors can provide students with options for how they will engage with the subject matter of a course. Students may choose skills-based forms of assessment or they may elect to write a seminar essay, which has been an ineluctable component of content-driven models.

In other words, one does not need to abandon the discipline's signature pedagogy. To the contrary, an instructor can work closely with those students who have enthusiastically selected it as the basis for their assessment.

To provide the seminar essay as an option rather than a fixed requirement, however, is to acknowledge that a singular, summative form of assessment is not for everyone.

NOTES

1. The focus of this chapter is on graduate seminars taught during regular academic terms (either a semester or quarter). For a consideration of graduate-level assignments in the context of short-term study abroad programs with condensed timeframes and experiential components, see Morrison 2019.

2. Giving students a choice of assessment options contributes to an autonomy-supportive classroom. On the links among autonomy, motivation, and learning, see Chang et al. 2017, 99–110.

3. As Cassuto (2015) notes, advocates of student-centered learning have made their case since at least "John Dewey and Jean Piaget" (67). In fact, one could argue that the idea dates back to Rousseau's *Émile*, in which the philosophe proposes "the parent-tutor as facilitator, who does not dictate what a child should learn, but rather permits a significant degree of autonomy for experiential learning" (Morrison 2018, 3).

Coda

Demystifying the Seminar Paper
Jessie Reeder

Halfway through my first semester of graduate school, I heard the term "seminar paper" for the first time, and I was thoroughly mystified. I understood the general mandate to write twenty pages of prose. But the length of the assignment seemed to be the only piece of information any of my classmates required beyond the two words "seminar paper," which I quickly realized were, for the initiated, an entire writing prompt unto themselves. As an undergraduate, I was used to getting some concrete direction about my intended audience, the role of research, scope of topic, etc. But the nodding heads around the seminar table told me that I was the only *graduate* student who needed such guidance. (In retrospect, I am sure I was not.)

I thought there must simply be a piece of information others had gotten but I hadn't yet. But there wasn't. The seminar paper turned out to be a genre that students and faculty around me had variously attempted, practiced, absorbed, and intuited, but either could not or saw no need to explain. When I visited my professor and asked him how to write a seminar paper, he stared at me blinkingly before saying he didn't understand my question. "You can write about anything!" he said with perplexed annoyance, as though radical open-endedness were the solution to, not the source of, my problem. (It was a class on globalization, no less, so "anything" in this case was staggeringly literal.) Other faculty during the next few years were happy to talk with me about my *ideas* for seminar papers but were frustratingly unhelpful about the genre itself. In one memorable instance, a professor returned my rough draft with the first two pages—a painstakingly crafted précis of postmodernism—crossed out. Next to it he had written, "Everyone already knows this." Of course, *I* hadn't known it; that's why I did the research and reported my findings. All I learned from this experience was that "everyone" didn't include me, and that I had accidentally stumbled upon a wrong way to write a seminar paper but still didn't know the right one.

In the end, I muddled through. I practiced, I talked to my peers, I anatomized published articles, I decoded faculty feedback, and I figured it out. By the time I finished coursework I had, like most graduate students, I think, arrived at a loose, intuitive sense of what I was doing. But it wasn't until I began *teaching others* that my understanding of the seminar paper became more conscious and precise. As both a writing center tutor in graduate school and a professor of graduate courses myself, I have had to figure out not just what a seminar paper feels like, but what it's actually trying to accomplish and how to explain that to someone else.

Seminar papers are especially challenging for new graduate students because the difference from undergraduate writing is not just one of scale: it's one of purpose. Whereas the undergraduate essay typically produces an analysis, the graduate seminar paper is more often expected to *contribute to a conversation*. Bundled along with that difference comes a whole host of corresponding shifts the writer must make: the intended audience, the amount and purpose of research, the role of the text, the scale of the claim, and the overall structure of the essay, all of which likely place new graduate writers in unfamiliar territory. It may well be obvious to them that the journal articles they are reading for class look very different than the ten-page college essays they've become adept at writing, but recognizing a difference is not the same as knowing how to replicate it.

Of course, while some early career graduate students will never have written anything longer than a dozen pages, others will have written long research papers in college. But even those who have written a sixty-page senior thesis are unlikely to intuitively grasp the compact scale required by the twenty-page disciplinary intervention that a seminar paper is meant to be. Gone are the ten-page literature review, extended preamble, and fifty-source bibliography that their thesis likely featured, nor will they have four to eight months to write it. Most graduate students taking coursework face the alarming task of producing more or less a competent draft of a journal article (a genre they have likely never written before), often on a subject that is at best tangential to their interests, usually in a few days' time, and under the pressure of impressing future advisers and recommenders. These are not ideal conditions for learning the craft of writing.

The goal of this handout is to begin the process of demystifying the seminar paper. It is an attempt to distill its constitutive elements into concrete steps a writer can pursue—to construct a bridge across what can seem like a chasm between a writer and a new genre. Some things are explicit here, and others are implicit. I do not take for granted that any or all of the processes on this handout will be obvious to a student or come naturally. For instance, "finding a gap in a critical conversation" may be a new idea that requires explanation, modeling, and practice. Moreover, this handout offers concrete steps toward *developing a viable seminar paper idea*; it does not venture into the writing process itself, nor does it offer suggestions for organizing a seminar paper. This document, therefore, is not intended to replace writing instruction in the graduate classroom; rather, it's meant to *propel* it. It is a primer on the skills a seminar paper writer may need and that faculty certainly should help them acquire.

Some (even a lot of) confusion and apprehension are built into a writer's growth: learning new genres almost always produces a vertiginous sense of returning to beginnerdom. I do not want to suggest otherwise. But we shouldn't ask students to find their way through that struggle on their own or by trial and error. Nor should we assume that students who don't ask for help don't need it. I find graduate students exceptionally eager for the demystification of academic genres, but I frequently discover this only after initiating a conversation about writing. I worry that academic culture often sends the message to graduate students that they should already know how to produce its genres, and that if they don't, the ability to figure it out on their own is a test of their suitability for the profession. That's not a healthy dynamic for our supposed apprenticeship model. Writers never stop learning how to write, and graduate teachers have an obligation to help them.

DEVELOPING A SUCCESSFUL SEMINAR PAPER

The following are suggested steps for developing a graduate seminar paper. Without being prescriptive or exhaustive, they are nonetheless meant to demystify this genre and its production. I recommend you take each one slowly in turn. But keep in mind that your process won't always be linear. For instance, familiarizing yourself with a theoretical conversation (step 5) may help you develop ideas for steps 1–3 that you wouldn't otherwise have had. Likewise, after completing step 4, you may realize your question has already been answered satisfactorily, sending you back to step 1. These steps were crafted with a literary studies essay in mind, but they may well be useful in other disciplines.

1. Choose a _text and topic_: Your topic could be formal, thematic, or a combination of the two. For example, *The Purple Cloud* + [race] or [temporal discontinuity] or [social obligation] or . . . Charlotte Smith's sonnets + [female labor] or [enjambment] or [selfhood] or . . . *Adventures of Mrs. Seacole* + [limits of dissent] or [politics of caretaking] or . . .
2. Establish a _focal point_: What's odd, unique, prominent, generative, unsettling, or paradoxical about the way the text deals with this topic? Why is it worth looking at? (Not every text and topic is.)
3. Pose a _question_: What question(s) does that focal point raise? Your question should not have an obvious answer, and if you aren't sure what you think the answer is, even better. Try to ask a question with *stakes*—a question whose answer will matter to others in your field.
4. Find a gap in the _critical conversation_: Have critics who've written about this text noticed this same focal point? Have they asked this same question? If not, why not? If so, how have they answered it? What remains unsaid (or unsatisfactory about what has been said)?
5. Situate yourself in a _theoretical conversation_: By asking this question, what theoretical conversation(s) are you entering into? (e.g., historical materialism, queer theory, narratology, etc.). How will using this theory help you answer your question in a new and interesting way?
6. Develop an _argument_ about the text: With your theoretical conversation in mind, close read your text through the lens of your focal point. Develop an answer to the question(s) you asked. This answer should

constitute a new and original claim about how the text operates, the ideas it expresses, or its relation to its context.
7. Pose a *response to the theory*: How does your argument reveal the theory you used to be itself incomplete What do you have to say to scholars in that conversation?

These are the stages of *developing a paper*. Writing the paper itself is a further process. A paper proposal should reflect some good, thoughtful work on steps 1 through 5. It is not necessary to have read all of the criticism on your text (element 4) at the proposal stage. However, you should be reasonably sure that you are in fact headed toward an original claim that has not been made before. A good final paper for a graduate seminar will display the results of steps 1–6. A paper that is on its way to becoming a publishable article will have passed carefully through all seven steps.

References

ADE [Association of Departments of English] Ad Hoc Committee on the Master's Degree. 2001. *Rethinking the Master's Degree in English for a New Century*. New York: Modern Language Association.

Alemán, Mateo. 2001. *Guzmán de Alfarache*. 1599, 1604. Edited by José Maria Micó. Madrid: Editorial Cátedra.

Alemán, Mateo. 1967. *The Rogue, or the Life of Guzmán de Alfarache*. 1622. Edited by James Fitzmaurice-Kelly and translated by James Mabbe. 1924. Reprint, New York: AMS Press.

Anderson, Mike. 2016. *Learning to Choose, Choosing to Learn: The Key to Student Motivation and Achievement*. Alexandria, VA: ASCD.

Andrews, Richard. 2007. "Argumentation, Critical Thinking and the Postgraduate Dissertation." *Educational Review* 59, no. 1 (February): 1–18.

Andrews, Richard. 2003. "The End of the Essay?" *Teaching in Higher Education* 8, no. 1: 117–28. doi: 10.1080/1356251032000052366.

Anker, Elizabeth S., and Rita Felski. 2017. Introduction to *Critique and Postcritique*, edited by Elizabeth S. Anker and Rita Felski, 1–28. Durham, NC: Duke University Press.

Bacon, Francis. 1625. *The Essayes or Counsels, Civill and Morall*. London: Early English Books Online.

Badenhorst, Cecile, Cecilia Moloney, Janna Rosales, Jennifer Dyer, and Lina Ru. 2015. "Beyond Deficit: Graduate Student Research-Writing Pedagogies." *Teaching in Higher Education* 20, no. 1: 1–11. doi: 10.1080/13562517.2014.945160.

Badley, Graham. 2009. "Academic Writing as Shaping and Re-Shaping." *Teaching in Higher Education* 14, no. 2: 209–19. doi: 10.1080/13562510902757294.

Badley, Graham. 2010. "Valuing Essays: Essaying Values." *Research in Post-Compulsory Education* 15, no. 1: 103–15. doi: 10.1080/13596740903565434.

Bakhtin, M. M. "Discourse in the Novel." 1992. In *The Dialogic Imagination: Four Essays*, edited by Michael Holquist and translated by Caryl Emerson and Michael Holquist, 259–422. Austin: University of Texas Press.

Ballenger, Bruce. 2017. *The Curious Researcher: A Guide to Writing Research Papers*. 9th ed. Boston: Pearson.

Barnes, Christopher. 2015. "The Ideal Work Schedule, as Determined by Circadian Rhythms." *Harvard Business Review*. Last modified January 28, 2015, https://hbr.org/2015/01/the-ideal-work-schedule-as-determined-by-circadian-rhythms.

Bawarshi, Anis S., and Mary Jo Reiff. 2010. *Genre: An Introduction to History, Theory, Research, and Pedagogy*. West Lafayette, IN: Parlor Press and The WAC Clearinghouse.

Bechdel, Alison. 2006. *Fun Home: A Family Tragicomic*. Boston: Houghton Mifflin.

Benedek, András. "SysBook as a Visual Learning Frame." 2016. In *In the Beginning was the Image: The Omnipresence of Pictures*, edited by András Benedek and Ágnes Veszelszki, 161–70. New York: Lang.

Black, Scott. 2006. *Of Essays and Reading in Early Modern Britain*. Basingstoke: Palgrave Macmillan.

Blake-Hedges, Caitlyn. 2019. "We're All Frauds: Managing Imposter Syndrome in Grad School." *ASCB: An International Forum for Cell Biology*, March 30, 2018, accessed September 6, 2019, https://www.ascb.org/careers/frauds-managing-imposter-syndrome-grad-school/.

Blamires, Harry. 1991. *A History of Literary Criticism*. London: Macmillan.

Bourdieu, Pierre. 1977. *Outline of a Theory of Practice*. Translated by Richard Nice. Cambridge: Cambridge University Press.

Brodkey, Linda. 1987. *Academic Writing as Social Practice*. Philadelphia: Temple University Press.

Brookbank, Elizabeth, and H. Faye Christenberry. 2019. *MLA Guide to Undergraduate Research in Literature*. New York: Modern Language Association of America.

Brown, Sally and Peter Knight. 1994. *Assessing Learners in Higher Education*. London: Kogan and Page.

Burke, Kenneth. 1973. *The Philosophy of Literary Form: Studies in Symbolic Action*. 1941. 3rd ed. Berkeley: University of California Press.

Caffarella, Rosemary S., and Bruce G. Barnett. 2000. "Teaching Doctoral Students to Become Scholarly Writers: The Importance of Giving and Receiving Critiques." *Studies in Higher Education* 25, no. 1: 39–52. doi: 10.1080/030750700116000.

Caplan, Nigel A, and Michelle Cox. 2016. "The State of Graduate Communication Support: Results of an International Survey." In *Supporting Graduate Student*

Writers: Research, Curriculum, and Program Design, edited by Steve Simpson, Nigel A. Caplan, Michelle Cox, and Talinn Philips, 22–51. Ann Arbor: University of Michigan Press.

Carol Berkenkotter, Thomas Huckin, and John Ackerman. 1988. "Conventions, Conversations, and the Writer: Case Study of a Student in a Rhetoric Ph.D. Program." *Research in the Teaching of English* 22, no. 1: 9–44.

Casey, John. 2006. "Six Tips for Better Time Management." *WebMD*. Last modified July 24, 2006, https://www.webmd.com/add-adhd/features/time-management-tips#2.

Cassuto, Leonard. 1999. "Pressures to Publish Fuel the Professionalization of Today's Graduate Students." *The Chronicle of Higher Education* 45, no. 14: B4.

Cassuto, Leonard. 2015. *The Graduate School Mess: What Caused It and How We Can Fix It*. Cambridge, MA: Harvard University Press.

Chang, Rong, et al. 2017. "Enhancing Students' Motivation with Autonomy-Supportive Classrooms." In *Development of Self-Determination Through the Life-Course*, edited by Michael L. Wehmeyer et al., 99–110. Dordrecht: Springer.

Chesterton, Gilbert Keith. 2000. *On Lying in Bed and Other Essays by G. K. Chesterton*. Edited by Alberto Manguel. Calgary: Bayeux Arts.

Clark, Irene L. 2006. *Writing the Successful Thesis and Dissertation: Entering the Conversation*. Upper Saddle River, NJ: Prentice Hall.

Clark, William. 2006. *Academic Charisma and the Origins of the Research University*. Chicago: University of Chicago Press.

"Communicating with English Language Learners." 2018. *Remind.com*. Last modified 2018, https://assets.remind.com/marketing/pdfs/remind-communicating-with-english-language-learners.pdf.

Conomos, John. 2016. "The Self-Portrait and the Film and Video Essay." In *Imaging Identity: Media, Memory and Portraiture in the Digital Age*, edited by Melinda Hinkson, 85–100. Canberra, Australia: ANU Press.

Cope, Bill, and Mary Kalantzis. 2005. "Multiliteracies–A Pedagogy of Multiliteracies: Designing social futures–The New London Group." In *Multiliteracies: Literacy Learning and the Design of Social Futures*, 9–40. New York: Routledge.

Cope, Bill, and Mary Kalantzis. 2015. "The Things You Do to Know: An Introduction to the Pedagogy of Multiliteracies." In *A Pedagogy of Multiliteracies Learning*, edited by B. Cope and M. Kalantzis, 1–36. Basingstoke: Palgrave Macmillan.

Crane, Ronald. 1968. "The Relation of Bacon's Essays to the Program of the Advancement of Learning." In *Essential Articles for the Study of Francis Bacon*, edited by Brian Vickers, 272–92. Hamden, CT: Archon Books.

Curry, Mary Jane. 2016. "More Than Language: Graduate Student Writing as 'Disciplinary Becoming.'" In *Supporting Graduate Student Writers: Research, Curriculum, and Program Design*, edited by Steve Simpson, Nigel A. Caplan, Michelle Cox, and Talinn Philips, 78–96. Ann Arbor: University of Michigan Press.

CWPA. 2014. "WPA Outcomes Statement for First-Year Composition (v3.0)." http://wpacouncil.org/positions/outcomes.html.

CWPA, NCTE, NWP. 2011. "Framework for Success in Postsecondary Writing." http://wpacouncil.org/framework.

Davis, Barbara Gross. 1993. *Tools for Teaching*. San Francisco: Jossey-Bass.

Delgado, Richard. 1992. "The Imperial Scholar Revisited: How to Marginalize Outsider Writing, Ten Years Later." *University of Pennsylvania Law Review* 140, no. 4 (April): 1349–72. https://www.jstor.org/stable/3312406.

Digdon, Nancy. 2010. "Circadian preference and college students' beliefs about sleep education." *Chronobiology International: The Journal of Biological and Medical Rhythm Research* 27, no. 2: 297–317. doi: 10.3109/07420520903502895.

Dobie, Ann B. 2012. *Theory into Practice: An Introduction to Literary Criticism*. 3rd ed. Boston: Wadsworth Cengage Learning.

Durant, Alan, and Nigel Fabb. 2016. *How to Write Essays and Dissertations: A Guide for English Literature Students*. New York: Routledge.

Eisenman, R. 2002. "Some Realities of Book Reviewing." *Journal of Information Ethics* 11, no. 1: 22–25.

Eliot, T. S. 2003. "Tradition and the Individual Talent." 1919. In *The Norton Anthology of Modern and Contemporary Poetry*. Vol. 1. 3rd ed. Edited by Jahan Ramazani, Richard Ellmann, and Robert O'Clair, 941–47. New York: Norton.

Fennis, Bob M., and Wolfgang Stroebe. 2010. *The Psychology of Advertising*. Hove: Psychology Press.

Flaherty, Colleen. 2018. "The Evolving English Major." *Inside Higher Ed*, July 18, accessed September 4, 2019, https://www.insidehighered.com/news/2018/07/18/new-analysis-english-departments-says-numbers-majors-are-way-down-2012-its-not-death.

"Four Ways to Make the Most of Your Professor's Office Hours." *Campus Explorer*. https://www.campusexplorer.com/college-advice-tips/17ED0E8E/4-Ways-to-Make-the-Most-of-Your-Professors-Office-Hours/.

Freadman, Anne. 2002. "Uptake." In *The Rhetoric and Ideology of Genre: Strategies for Stability and Change*, edited by Richard M. Coe, Lorelei Lingard, and Tatiana Teslenko, 39–53. Cresskill, NJ: Hampton Press.

Freedman, Aviva, and Christine Adam. 1996. "Learning to Write Professionally: 'Situated Learning' and the Transition from University to Professional Discourse." *Journal of Business and Technical Communication* 10, no. 4: 395–427.

Freedman, Diane P., Olivia Frey, and Frances Murphy Zauhar, eds. 1993. *The Intimate Critique: Autobiographical Literary Criticism*. Durham, NC: Duke University Press.

Gigante, Denise. 2014. "Introduction: The Essay; An Attempt; a Protean Form." *Republics of Letters* 4, no. 1: 1–14.

Gigante, Denise. 2010. "Sometimes a Stick is Just a Stick: The Essay as (Organic) Form." *European Romantic Review* 21, no. 5: 553–65.

Graff, Gerald, and Cathy Birkenstein. 2018. *They Say / I Say: The Moves That Matter in Academic Writing*. 4th ed. New York: Norton.

Gray, Floyd. 1999. "The Essay as Criticism." In *The Cambridge History of Literary Criticism: Volume III, The Renaissance*, edited by Glyn P. Norton, 271–77. Cambridge: Cambridge University Press.

Greenwald, Anthony G. 1968. "Cognitive Learning, Cognitive Response to Persuasion, and Attitude Change." In *Psychological Foundations of Attitudes*, edited by Anthony G. Greenwald, Timothy C. Brock, and Thomas M. Ostrom, 147–70. Amsterdam: Academic Press.

Hall, Susanne, and Jonathan Dueck. 2016. "Editors' Introduction: Presenting Writing Assignments as Intellectual Work and as Disciplinary Practice." *Prompt: A Journal of Academic Writing Assignments* 1, no. 1. doi: 10.31719/pjaw.v1i1.9.

Halpern, Faye, and James Phelan. 2017. "Writing an Effective Abstract: An Audience-Based Approach." *Inside Higher Ed*, February 23, accessed September 1, 2019, https://www.insidehighered.com/advice/2017/02/23/importance-writing-effective-abstract-when-you-submit-journal-article-essay.

Harris, Joseph. 2006. *Rewriting: How to Do Things with Texts*. Logan: Utah State University Press.

Harris, Martha Jane. 2006. "Three Steps to Teaching Abstract and Critique Writing." *International Journal of Teaching and Learning in Higher Education*. https://www.researchgate.net/publication/242520270.

Hayot, Eric. 2014. *The Elements of Academic Style: Writing for the Humanities*. New York: Columbia University Press.

Hazlitt, William Carew. 1877. "Preface to The Essays of Montaigne". In Michel de Montaigne, Charles Cotton, and William Carew Hazlitt. *The Essays of Montaigne*. London: Reeves and Turner. Accessed 10 August 2019, https://www.gutenberg.org/files/3600/3600-h/3600-h.htm

Hodgson, John and Ann Harris. 2013. "'It is Hard to Know What You are Being asked to do.' Deciphering Codes, Constructing Schemas." *English in Education* 47, no. 1: 6–17.

Howson, Alexandra. 2008. "Visual Matters in Learning and Teaching." *Learning and Teaching: The International Journal of Higher Education in the Social Sciences* 1, no. 3: 43–66.

Hyland, Ken. 2002. "Authority and Invisibility: Authorial Identity in Academic Writing." *Journal of Pragmatics* 34, no. 8 (August): 1092–112. doi: 10.1016/S0378-2166(02)00035-8.

Ivanič, Roz. 1998. *Writing and Identity: The Discoursal Construction of Identity in Academic Writing*. Philadelphia, PA: John Benjamins.

Janiszewski, Chris. 1990. "The Influence of Print Advertisement Organization on Affect toward a Brand Name." *Journal of Consumer Research* 17, no. 1: 53–65.

Jewitt, Carey. 2008. "Multimodality and Literacy in School Classrooms." *Review of Research In Education* 32, no. 1: 241–67.

Johnson, Samuel. 1778. Preface. *The Plays of William Shakespeare*. Vol. 1. 2nd ed., 1–67. London: Printed for C. Bathurst et al., accessed September 3, 2019, https://babel.hathitrust.org/cgi/pt?id=hvd.hxgex4&view=1up&seq=13.

Jones, Adrian N. 2018. "A (Theory and Pedagogy) Essay on the (History) Essay." *Arts and Humanities in Higher Education* 17, no. 2: 222–40.

Kellner, Douglas. 2019. "Multiple Literacies and Critical Pedagogy in a Multicultural Society." Accessed 10 May 2019, http://www.gseis.ucla.edu/faculty/kellner/.

Kelsky, Karen. 2015. *The Professor is In: The Essential Guide to Turning Your Ph.D. Into a Job*. New York: Three Rivers Press.

Khost, Peter H., Debra Rudder Lohe and Chuck Sweetman. 2015. "Rethinking and Unthinking the Graduate Seminar." *Pedagogy* 15, no. 1: 19–30.

Kibbe, Michael. 2016. *From Topic to Thesis: A Guide to Theological Research*. Downers Grove, IL: InterVarsity Press.

Kress, Gunther, and Theo Van Leeuwen. 2001. *Multimodal Discourse: The Modes and Media of Contemporary Communication*. London: Arnold.

Lavelle, Ellen, and Kathy Bushrow. 2007. "Writing Approaches of Graduate Students." *Educational Psychology* 27, no. 6: 807–22. doi: 10.1080/01443410701366001.

Lawrence, Susan, and Terry Myers Zawacki, eds. 2019. *Re/Writing the Center: Approaches to Supporting Graduate Students in the Writing Center*. Logan: Utah State University Press.

Lewis, Arthur, and David Smith. 1993. "Defining higher order thinking." *Theory into Practice* 32, no. 3: 131–37.

Lundell, Dana Britt, and Richard Beach. 2003. "Dissertation Writers' Negotiations with Competing Activity Systems." In *Writing Selves, Writing Societies: Research from Activity Perspectives*, edited by Charles Bazerman and David R. Russell, 483–514. Fort Collins, CO: WAC Clearinghouse.

Mack, Peter. 2010. *Reading and Rhetoric in Montaigne and Shakespeare*. London: Bloomsbury.

Malaysian Qualifications Agency. 2014. *Guidelines to Good Practices: Monitoring, Reviewing and Continually Improving Institutional Quality*.

Mall, Kristy. 2012. "Are You Reaching Your Digital Natives?" *Scholastic*. Last modified February 12, 2012, https://www.scholastic.com/teachers/blog-posts/kristy-mall/are-you-reaching-your-digital-natives/.

Marken, Stephanie. 2019. "A Crisis of Confidence in Higher Ed." *Gallup*, April 12, 2019, accessed September 4, 2019, https://news.gallup.com/opinion/gallup/248492/crisis-confidence-higher.aspx.

Mattiuozzi, Robert N., and Elizabeth Blakesley Lindsay. 2008. *Literary Research and the American Modernist Era: Strategies and Sources*. Lanham, MD: Scarecrow Press.

McCarthy, John. 1989. *Crossing Boundaries: A Theory and History of Essay Writing in German 1680–1915*. Philadelphia: University of Pennsylvania Press.

McCullough, Kate. 2018. "'The Complexity of Loss Itself': The Comics Form and *Fun Home*'s Queer Reparative Temporality." *American Literature* 90, no. 2 (June): 377–405. https://doi-org.proxygt-law.wrlc.org/10.1215/00029831-4564346.

McTighe, Jay, and Grant Wiggins. 2013. *Essential Questions: Opening Doors to Student Understanding*. Alexandria, VA: ASCD.

Micciche, Laura R., and Allison Carr. 2011. "Toward Graduate Level Writing Instruction." *College Composition and Communication* 62, no. 3: 477–501.

Miller, Carolyn R. 1984. "Genre as Social Action." *Quarterly Journal of Speech* 70, no. 2: 151–67.

"MLA International Bibliography." 2019. Modern Language Association, accessed September 6, 2019, https://www.mla.org/Publications/MLA-International-Bibliography.

Modern Language Association. 2014. "Report of the MLA Task Force on Doctoral Study in Modern Language and Literature." *Web Publication*.

Montaigne, Michel Eyquem de. 2007. *Les Essais*, edited by Jean Balsamo, Michel Magnien and Catherine Magnien-Simonin. Paris: Éditions Gallimard.

Morrison, Kevin A. 2018. *A Micro-History of Victorian Liberal Parenting: John Morley's "Discreet Indifference."* Cham: Palgrave.

Morrison, Kevin A. 2019. *Study Abroad Pedagogy, Dark Sites, and Historical Reenactment: In the Footsteps of Jack the Ripper and His Victims*. Cham: Palgrave.

Nelson, Cary. 2011. *No University is an Island: Saving Academic Freedom*. New York: NYU Press.

Nguyen, Ryan. 2011. "Make the Most Out of Office Hours." *College Info Geek*. Last modified September 8, 2011, https://collegeinfogeek.com/make-the-most-out-of-office-hours/.

Obaldia, Claire de. 1995. *The Essayistic Spirit: Literature, Modern Criticism, and the Essay*. Oxford: Clarendon Press.

Obeng-Odoom, Franklin. 2014. "Why Write Book Reviews." *Australian Universities' Review* 56, no. 1: 78–82.

OED Online. June 2019. s.v. "Criticism, n." accessed September 2, 2019, https://www-oed-com.proxygt-law.wrlc.org/view/Entry/44598?redirectedFrom=criticism#eid.

Oinas, P., and Leppälä, S. 2013. "Views on Book Reviews." *Regional Studies*, 47, no. 10: 1785–89.

Okahana, Hironao, and Enyu Zhou. 2018. "Graduate Enrollment and Degrees: 2007 to 2017." Washington, DC: Council of Graduate Schools.

Pantenburg, Volker. 2015. "Deviation as Norm – Notes on the Essay Film." In *Farocki/Godard: Film as Theory*, edited by Volker Pantenburg, 135–52. Amsterdam: Amsterdam University Press.

Pfister, Joel. 2000. "Complicity Critiques." *American Literary History* 12, no. 3 (Autumn): 610–32. http://www.jstor.org.proxygt-law.wrlc.org/stable/490225.

Phelan, James, and Faye Halpern. 2018. "Writing Effective Journal Essay Introductions." *Inside Higher Ed*, May 16, accessed September 5, 2019, https://www.insidehighered.com/advice/2018/05/16/how-craft-introductions-journal-essays-opinion.

Poe, Mya, Neal Lerner, and Jennifer Craig. 2010. *Learning to Communicate in Science and Engineering: Case Studies from MIT*. Cambridge, MA: MIT Press.

Price, Margaret. 2011. *Mad at School: Rhetorics of Mental Disability and Academic Life*. Ann Arbor: University of Michigan Press.

Prince, Michael. 2004. "Does Active Learning Work? A Review of the Research." *Journal of Engineering Education* 93, no. 3: 223–31.

Prior, Paul A. 1998. *Writing/Disciplinarity: A Sociohistoric Account of Literate Activity in the Academy*. New York: Routledge.

Pugh, Tison, and Margaret E. Johnson. 2014. *Literary Studies: A Practical Guide*. Abingdon: Routledge.

Purdue *OWL*. https://owl.purdue.edu/owl/general_writing/mechanics/hocs_and_locs.html.

Race, Philip et al. 2005. *500 Tips on Assessment*. London: Routledge-Falmer.

Ramazani, Jahan. 2012. "Contemporary Poetry." Fall Syllabus, University of Virginia, Charlottesville, VA (on file with author).

Rascaroli, Laura. 2008. "The Essay Film: Problems, Definitions, Textual Commitments." *Framework* 49, no. 2: 24–47.

Ricoeur, Paul. 1970. *Freud & Philosophy: An Essay on Interpretation*, translated by Denis Savage. New Haven, CT: Yale University Press.

Roberts, Jennifer L. 2013. "The Power of Patience." *Harvard Magazine* (November–December): 40–43.

Roes, Remco, and Kris Pint. 2017. "The Visual Essay and the Place of Artistic Research in the Humanities." *Pelgrave Communications* 3, no. 8: 1–7.

Rose, Mike, and Karen A McClafferty. 2001. "A Call for the Teaching of Writing in Graduate Education." *Educational Researcher* 30, no. 2: 27–33.

Sambell, Kay, Liz McDowell, and Catherine Montgomery. 2013. *Assessment for Learning in Higher Education*. London: Routledge.

Scharper, Julie. 2018. "Are You Addicted to Your Phone?" *Scholastic*. Last modified February 2018, https://choices.scholastic.com/issues/2017-18/020118/are-you-addicted-to-your-phone-.html.

Sedgwick, Eve Kosofsky. 1997. "Paranoid Reading and Reparative Reading; or, You're So Paranoid, You Probably Think This Introduction Is about You." In *Novel Gazing: Queer Readings in Fiction*, edited by Eve Kosofsky Sedgwick, 1–37. Durham, NC: Duke University Press.

Semenza, Gregory M. Colón. 2010. *Graduate Study for the Twenty-First Century: How to Build an Academic Career in the Humanities*. New York: Palgrave.

Shakespeare, William. 1984. *Macbeth*. Edited by Kenneth Muir. London: Methuen.

Simpson, Steve, Nigel A Caplan, Michelle Cox, Talinn Philips, and Steve Simpson. 2016. *Supporting Graduate Student Writers: Research, Curriculum, and Program Design*. Ann Arbor: University of Michigan Press.

Spacks, Patricia Meyer. 1994. "The Academic Marketplace: Who Pays Its Costs?" *MLA Newsletter* 26, no. 2: 3.

Spector, Robert Donald. 1997. *Samuel Johnson and the Essay*. Westport, CT: Greenwood Press.

"Spending Less Time on Guesswork." 2018. *Asana*. Last modified 2018, https://asana.com/.

Spivak, Gayatri Chakravorty. 2012. *An Aesthetic Education in the Era of Globalization*. Cambridge, MA: Harvard University Press.

Spivak, Gayatri Chakravorty. 2008. *Other Asias*. Oxford: Blackwell.

Starke-Meyerring, Doreen. 2011. "The Paradox of Writing in Doctoral Education: Student Experiences." In *Doctoral Education: Research-Based Strategies for Doctoral Students, Supervisors and Administrators*, edited by Lynn McAlpine and Cheryl Amundsen, 75–95. Dordrecht; New York: Springer.

Steen, Sara, Chris Bader, and Charis Kubrin. 1999. "Rethinking the Graduate Seminar." *Teaching Sociology* 27, no. 2: 167–73.

Straumann, Barbara. 2015. "Adaptation – Remediation – Transmediality." In *Handbook of Intermediality: Literature – Image – Sound – Music*, edited by Gabriele Rippl, 249–67. Berlin: DeGruyter.

Sword, Helen. 2012. *Stylish Academic Writing*. Cambridge, MA: Harvard University Press.

Sword, Helen. 2016. *The Writer's Diet: A Guide to Fit Prose*. Chicago: University of Chicago Press.

Sullivan, Patricia A. 1991. "Writing in the Graduate Curriculum: Literary Criticism as Composition." *Journal of Advanced Composition* 11, no. 2: 283–99.

Vargas Llosa, Mario. 2015. *Notes on the Death of Culture: Essays on Spectacle and Society*, translated by John King. New York: Farrar, Straus and Giroux.

Vozza, Stephanie. 2013. "Time Blocking: A Productivity Tool." *Entrepreneur*. Last modified April 8, 2013. https://www.entrepreneur.com/article/226231.

Wallace, Mike, and Alison Wray. 2016. *Critical Reading and Writing for Postgraduates*. 3rd ed. Thousand Oaks, CA: Sage Publications.

Wallack, Nicole B. 2017. *Crafting Presence: The American Essay and the Future of Writing Studies*. Boulder: University Press of Colorado.

Weissbourd, Emily. 2017 "Translating Spain: Purity of Blood and Orientalism in Mabbe's *Rogue* and *Guzmán de Alfarache*." *Modern Philology* 144, no. 3 (February): 552–72. https://doi.org/10.1086/688623.

"What is Asana?" 2017. *Blackbox Social Media*. Last accessed 2017, http://blackbox-socialmedia.com/how-does-asana-work/.

Wilde, Oscar. 1982. "The Critic as Artist." In *The Artist as Critic: Critical Writings of Oscar Wilde*, edited by Richard Ellmann, 341–408. Chicago: University of Chicago Press.

Womack, Peter. 1993. "What are Essays for?" *English in Education* 27, no. 2: 42–49.

Wood, Michael. 2014. "No Success Like Failure: Borges inside the Essay." *Republics of Letters* 4, no. 1: 1–6.

Woolf, Virginia. 1994. *The Essays of Virginia Woolf, Vol IV: 1925–1928*, edited by Andrew McNeillie. London: The Hogarth Press.

Woolf, Virginia. 2002. "The Modern Essay." In *The Common Reader*. First Series. 1925. Boston: Mariner Books.

"Wunderlist: To-Do Lists and Tasks." 2018. *Apple Inc.* Last modified 2018, https://itunes.apple.com/us/app/wunderlist-to-do-list-tasks/id406644151?mt=8.

Yagoda, Ben. 2013. *How to Not Write Bad: The Most Common Writing Problems and the Best Ways to Avoid Them*. New York. Riverhead.

Index

academic job market, 3, 5, 20, 31, 101, 102, 164, 167
Addison, Joseph, 17
Adorno, Theodor, 19, 144
advertising and advertisements, 134–39, 160
Alemán, Mateo, *Guzmán de Alfarache*, 53–54
Andrews, Richard, 23, 155, 158
Angelou, Maya, 21
ANQ, 175
Aristotle, 16

Bacon, Francis, 14–16; *Advancement of Learning*, 14; *Essayes*, 15–16, 18
Bakhtin, Mikhail, 66; *The Dialogic Imagination*, 43
Barnes, Christopher, 89–90
Barnum, P. T., *The Life of P.T. Barnum*, 156, 158
Bechdel, Alison, *Fun Home: A Family Tragicomic*, 52–53
Belfast Telegraph, 136, 137
Benedek, András, 134, 143
Bense, Max, 19
Bhabha, Homi, 156–58
Biggs, John B., and Kevin F. Collis, 153–54
Bourdieu, Pierre, 24

The Brampton Guardian, 136
Brown, Sally, 166, 168
Burke, Kenneth, 46–47, 66, 67

Caffarella, Rosemary S., and Bruce G. Barnett, 62
Cambridge, Duchess of, 136
Cambridge Blog, 140, 141
careers, 8, 28, 75, 81, 86, 87, 99, 166
Casey, John, "Six Tips for Better Time Management," 91
Cassuto, Leonard, 9n2, 176, 177n3
Chesterton, G. K., 19
Clark, Irene, 44
Cognitive Response Model (CRM), 134, 135, 137
comprehensive examinations, 75, 163
conference papers, 3, 20, 29, 124, 126, 172–74
Conomos, John, 143
Conrad, Joseph, 158; *Heart of Darkness*, 156, 158
Consortium on Graduate Communication, 28
Cope, Bill, and Mary Kalantzis, 155–56
Cornwallis, William, 17, 19
Craig, Alexander, 17
Crane, Ronald, 16
CRM. *See* Cognitive Response Model

The Daily Telegraph, 136, 138
Davis, Barbara Gross, 167
de Obaldia, Claire, 19
Dewey, John, 177
digital humanities, 48
dissertation proposal, 58
dissertations, 1, 3–7, 21, 29, 40, 44, 45, 58–59, 86, 102, 167
doctoral students, 27–29, 33, 164–66
Durant, Alan, and Nigel Fabb, *How to Write Essays and Dissertations*, 6

Elbow, Peter, 67
Eliot, T. S.: "Tradition and the Individual Talent," 45
ELN, 175
Emerson, Ralph Waldo, 19
Erasmus, Desiderius, 16
essay: definitions of, 14–17; history of, 14–19; in Malaysia, 153–56; multimodal nature of, 149–50, 152, 157
essay films, 144
examinations, 5, 17, 18, 75, 76, 79, 81, 86, 100, 163
Explicator, 175

film editing, 147, 148
"Four Ways to Make the Most of Your Professor's Office Hours," 96, 97

grades and grading, 29–32, 36, 87, 96, 97
graduate programs, 1, 4–5, 9n2, 27, 37–39, 62, 75, 86, 87, 99, 100, 153, 164
the graduate seminar: and the visual essay, 133–48; demographics of, 2; goals of, 163; note-taking for, 7, 78–79, 82, 86; reading effectively in, 77–78; sequenced assignments of, 61, 64–66, 72, 169–71
the graduate seminar essay: annotated bibliography of, 64, 66, 68–69, 72, 169; assessment of, 13–26, 65, 109, 110, 150, 153–55, 157, 161, 163–77; and attribution, 23–24, 51; and the 'brain dump' stage, 85; and creating ethos, 57–59; and critical conversations, 9, 28, 44, 46–48, 50, 52–54, 110, 181, 182; definitions of, 28–30, 33; digital approaches to, 133–48; evaluation criteria of, 4, 31, 45, 65, 147, 172–73; feedback on, 36, 38, 71, 82, 87, 88, 100, 105–8, 110, 119, 170, 180; as a genre, 9, 14, 19, 27–40, 43, 44, 179–82; goals of, 37–38, 61, 83, 88; interventions in existing research of, 49–50; and literary criticism, 43–55, 165; motive for writing, 29–33; opportunities provided by, 24–25, 29, 30, 33, 53; organization strategies for, 75–77, 80–81, 85–86; and peer review, 35, 39, 71, 88, 99–113; and prior scholarship, 44, 50; publishability of, 2–6, 20, 30, 31, 45, 183; purpose of, 28–33, 37–38, 45; qualities of, 4; and relationships with faculty, 31, 33, 35, 78; and 'reverse outlining', 85; time management of, 5, 7, 9, 78, 82–85, 87, 89–97, 107; writing strategies for, 75–88; writing workshops for, 4, 5, 100, 104–5, 109, 166, 168
graduate seminar presentations, 115–30; handouts for, 115, 118, 126, 128, 181; planning methods of, 120–24; rehearsals for, 117, 119, 124–29
graduate students: and anxiety, 3, 30, 32, 34–37, 43, 63; and conveying authority, 24, 57–59, 108; and the dissertation proposal, 58; and English Studies, 57, 150; and guidance/direction, 6, 22, 27, 35, 36, 44, 75, 109, 151, 179; and the 'imposter syndrome', 51, 108, 110; and the myth of the lone writer, 106, 108, 112; and the myth of the writerly genius, 108, 110; perceptions of the seminar paper by, 28–37; and professional development, 4, 6, 35, 86–88; and publishing. *See* the graduate seminar essay; research/response journal of, 50, 64, 72, 79,

81–82, 169; resources for, 6–7, 9; and scaffolding scholarship, 39, 61–72, 101; and scholarly style, 30, 64; and self-care, 87–88; and smartphone applications, 94; and student–professor interactions, 34–35; and syllabi, 3, 30, 36, 45, 65, 89, 90, 96, 101, 161, 163; and visual prioritization, 89–91; and writing groups, 88, 99–104, 107, 109–13;
graduate writers, 27, 64, 99, 108–10, 180
graduate writing, liminal nature of, 28
graduate writing centers, 4
graduate writing workshops, 5, 104, 105
Graff, Gerald: and Cathy Birkenstein, 44, 104, 113n2; *They Say, I Say*, 109
Greenwald, Anthony G., 135

Hall, Susanne, and Jonathan Dueck, 71
Harris, Joseph, *Rewriting: How To Do Things With Texts*, 109
Hayot, Eric, 6
higher-order thinking and critical skills, 150
Howson, Alexandra, 138–39
the humanities, 3, 13, 32, 48, 75, 84, 86–88, 104, 149, 151, 152, 155, 164, 173; challenges to, 153; goals and values of, 25, 26
Huxley, Aldous, 19
hypertextuality, 157–59

images. *See* graduate seminar
Instagram, 133, 134

Jewitt, Carey, 159
Johnson, Samuel, 17, 46, 150–52; *The Idler*, 17; *The Rambler*, 17
journal articles, 4, 29, 43–46, 64, 86, 116, 124, 159, 175, 180
JSTOR, 68

Keller, Gary, 92
Kelsky, Karen, 172
Kipling, Rudyard, 21, 158; *Plain Tales from the Hill*, 156, 158

Knight, Peter, 168
Kress, Gunther, and Theo Van Leeuwen, 151–52

Lewis, Arthur, and David Smith, 150
Locke, John, 2
Lopate, Phillip, 147
The Lord of the Rings (movie), 142
Lucretius, 16
Lukács, Georg, 19, 144

Mabbe, James, *The Rogue*, 53–54
MAH. *See* Matching Activation Hypothesis
Malaysia: literary programs in, 153, 155; popular songs and music of, 160
Malaysian Qualifications Agency (MQA), 153–54; *Guidelines To Good Practices*, 154
Marlowe, Christopher, 54
Matching Activation Hypothesis (MAH), 134, 135, 137
McCarthy, John, 19
McCullough, Kate, "'The Complexity of Loss Itself'," 52–53
metacommentary, 104, 105, 110–11, 113n2
Mill, John Stuart, 2
MLA. *See* Modern Language Association
MLA *International Bibliography*, 50
Modern Language Association (MLA), 5
Montaigne, Michel de, 14–16, 143, 150–52; *Essais*, 15
MQA. *See* Malaysian Qualifications Agency
multimodality, 149–52, 155–60

New London Group, 155–56
Notes and Queries, 175

Parker-Bowles, Camilla, 136
pedagogy and pedagogies, 14, 25, 36, 38, 70, 101, 138, 149–52, 155, 159, 161

peer workshops. *See* graduate writing workshops
Piaget, Jean, 177
Plutarch, 16
Price, Margaret, *kairotic spaces*, 38
professionalization, 5–6, 29, 30, 33, 38, 100
Pugh, Tison, and Margaret E. Johnson, 9n2

Race, Philip, 166
Rascaroli, Laura, 143–44
research paper, 44, 77, 120, 125, 160, 169, 180
rhetorical choices, 104, 110–12
rhetorical skills and strategies, 15–17, 22, 51, 53, 55, 59, 104, 144
Rhodes Must Fall movement, 21
Ricoeur, Paul, 55n1
Roberts, Jennifer L., 170
Roes, Remco, and Kris Pint, 146
Rose, Mike, and Karen McClafferty, 71
Rousseau, Jean-Jacques, *Émile*, 177n3

Said, Edward, 156–58
Scharper, Julie, "Are You Addicted to Your Phone?," 93
scholarly community, 43, 62, 66, 68, 70, 71, 88
scholarly discourse, voice, writing style, 30, 59, 63, 64, 66
scholarly journals, 5, 29, 30, 47, 51–53, 68–70, 175
Sedgwick, Eve Kosofsky, 53
Semenza, Gregory Colón, 7
seminar. *See* the graduate seminar
seminar essay. *See* the graduate seminar essay
Seneca, 16
Shakespeare, William, 54, 142; *Macbeth*, 139–40, 142; *Romeo and Juliet*, 140–42
Snapchat, 134
SOLO. *See* Structure of Observed Learning Outcome
Spacks, Patricia Meyer, 5

Spinoza, Baruch, 19
Spivak, Gayatri Chakravorty, 152, 153, 156–58; *Other Asias*, 149
Starke-Meyerring, Doreen, 36
Steele, Richard, 17
Stephens, John, 17
Structure of Observed Learning Outcome (SOLO), 153–54, 157
Sullivan, Patricia, 38
Sword, Helen, *The Writer's Diet: A Guide to Fit Prose*, 109, 111–12, 113n3
SWOT (strengths, weaknesses, opportunities, threats) analysis, 121–22

theoretical frameworks for textual analysis, 45
Turill, Daniel, 17
Twitter, 133, 140, 141

universities, 4, 14, 17, 18, 21, 23, 25, 87, 88, 153, 163, 164, 167

Vargas Llosa, Mario, 46
visual charts, 120–23
visual classrooms. *See* the graduate seminar
visual essay. *See* the graduate seminar
Vozza, Stephanie, 92

Wales, Prince of, 136
Wallack, Nicole B., 9n2
Weissbourd, Emily, "Translating Spain," 53–54
William, Prince, 136
Wither, George, 17
Woolf, Virginia, 19, 150–52
writing for publication, 5, 7
writing seminars, 5

Yagoda, Ben, *How to Not Write Bad*, 112–13
YouTube, 134, 147

Zotero, 80–81

Contributors

Lisann Anders holds a PhD in American literature from the University of Zurich, Switzerland, where she has taught several courses using multimedial tools in her role as a teaching and research assistant.

Janet G. Auten taught a graduate pedagogy seminar from 2000 to 2017 at American University in Washington, D.C., where she also directed the university's Writing Center.

Lucinda Becker is an award-winning academic at the University of Reading, where she is professor of pedagogy in the Department of English Literature.

Mark Celeste is visiting assistant professor of English, rhetoric, and writing at Berry College.

Thomas Deans is professor of English and director of the Writing Center at the University of Connecticut.

Natalie M. Dorfeld is associate professor of English in the School of Arts and Communication at Florida Institute of Technology, where she teaches freshman composition and literature.

Marilyn Gray is founding director of the Graduate Writing Center at the University of California, Los Angeles.

Almas Khan, who holds a PhD in English from the University of Virginia and a JD with honors from the University of Chicago Law School, is an assistant director of the Center for Legal English at Georgetown University Law Center.

Gabriel Morrison is a PhD student in rhetoric and composition at the University of Connecticut.

Shanthini Pillai is associate professor in the Faculty of Social Sciences and Humanities and Associate Senior Research Fellow at the Institute of Ethnic Studies (KITA), National University of Malaysia (UKM).

Jessie Reeder is assistant professor of English at Binghamton University, specializing in nineteenth-century British literature, imperialism, and form.

Philip Robinson-Self teaches in academic practice at the University of York, UK.

Elizabeth Vogel is associate professor of English at Arcadia University, where she serves as coordinator of professional writing and teaches courses in literature, composition, composition theory, rhetorical theory, creative nonfiction, and memoir writing.

About the Editor

Kevin A. Morrison is Provincial Chair Professor in the School of Foreign Languages at Henan University. He is the author of several works, including most recently, *Study Abroad Pedagogy, Dark Tourism, and Historical Reenactment: In the Footsteps of Jack the Ripper and His Victims*, and editor—among other volumes—of the forthcoming *Victorian Culture and Experiential Learning: Historical Encounters in the Classroom*.

www.ingramcontent.com/pod-product-compliance
Lightning Source LLC
Chambersburg PA
CBHW052043300426
44117CB00012B/1958